Christianity
According to
the Wesleys

©1996 by Nancy Hildebrandt

Originally published by Epworth Press, London, 1956

Published by Baker Books
a division of Baker Book House Company
P.O. Box 6287, Grand Rapids, MI 49516-6287

Labyrinth Books is an imprint of Baker Book House Company.

Printed in the United States of America

Library of Congress Cataloging-in-Publication Data

Hildebrandt, Franz, b. 1909
    Christianity according to the Wesleys : the Harris Franklin Rall lectures, 1954, delivered at Garrett Biblical Institute, Evanston, Illinois / Franz Hildebrandt.
      p. cm.
    "A Labyrinth book."
    Includes bibliographical references and index.
    ISBN 0-8010-2110-3 (pbk.)
    1. Wesley, John, 1703–1791. 2. Methodist Church—Doctrines—History—18th century. 3. Methodist Church—Doctrines. 4. Wesley, Charles, 1707–1788. I. Title
BX8495.W5H5 1996
230′.7′0922—dc21
                                                96-37302

For information about academic books, resources for Christian leaders, and all new releases available from Baker Book House, visit our web site:
http://www.bakerbooks.com

To the people of God, called Methodists
at
Romsey Town, Cambridge
and
Nicolson Square, Edinburgh

Sing we then in Jesu's name,
Now as yesterday the same;
One in every time and place,
Full for all of truth and grace!

Contents

Note on Sources

Works indicates the fourteen-volume edition (1829) of John Wesley's works, *Letters* the Standard Edition (eight volumes). The journals of John and Charles Wesley are quoted according to dates. Unless Charles Wesley is noted specifically, it should be assumed that the journal cited is that of John Wesley. *M.H.B.* indicates the English *Methodist Hymn-Book* (London, 1933).

Author's Note

These lectures cannot claim to be more than a first, sketchy introduction to the theology of Wesley (without, in the main, discriminating between John and Charles). To those who know him they say nothing new; the others, of course, and the Methodists among them in particular, one would wish to convince at least that they ought to know him. For this purpose it seemed advisable to let Wesley speak freely for himself, even where he speaks against modern Methodism; but to keep in mind, and point out where necessary, that the last word about Christianity must be, here as always, not "according to the Wesleys," but "according to the Scriptures." The semi-homiletic style is chiefly due to the unregenerate nature of a preacher not really converted to academic garb, and can only partly be ascribed to the setting of the beautiful Garrett Chapel where the lectures were delivered, and to the generosity of those who had them recorded for me.

The hospitality of the Garrett Faculty and the Rall Lectures Committee, particularly of Dr. and Mrs. Rockwell C. Smith, I shall always remember with gratitude. To be associated with the name of Harris Franklin Rall, and to meet with him and Mrs. Rall in person, was a high privilege indeed. The visit to Garrett could not, of course, have come about without the instrumentality of our late Dean, Clarence Tucker Craig, whom Drew misses so greatly and whose mother honored me by her presence at the opening lecture.

Franz Hildebrandt
Drew University, Madison, NJ
Commencement, 1954

1

Scriptural

City Road Chapel in London was about the last thing that I saw in England before crossing the Atlantic for the first time in September 1953. I stood before the tombstone of John Wesley and read:

> This great light arose by the singular providence of God, to enlighten these nations, and to revive, enforce and defend the pure apostolic doctrines and practices of the primitive Church; which he continued to do by his writings and his labours for more than half a century; and to his inexpressible joy not only beheld their influence extending, and their efficacy witnessed, in the hearts and lives of many thousands, as well in the Western world as in these kingdoms; but also, far above all human power or expectation, lived to see provision made, by the singular grace of God, for their continuance and establishment, to the joy of future generations. Reader, if thou art constrained to bless the instrument, give God the glory!

This, in the quaint language of the epitaph, is a good definition of Wesley's place in history and in theology. It must be confessed that this place has yet to be recognized; and Methodists must, alas, be the first to make their confession. Turn up any index of any modern theological book, and you will find, as a matter of course, Luther and Calvin, together with the great names of the present generation; but it almost goes without saying that you will look for the Wesleys in vain. Turn to the list of books which, I believe, local preachers are required to read in the Methodist Church in America; and although it would be a great shame if Dr. Rall did not figure as one of the four authors in question, he would, I know, be the first to admit the even greater shame that John Wesley, again, is not among them. And yet, when you consider the key position that he holds as a mediator between Luther and Calvin; between the Anglican mother Church and British Nonconformity; more importantly, between the age of the Reformation and the twentieth century; and last, but not least, between the tradition of the German Church and Western Christendom—it is clear that his place in theology alone could fill a whole lecture.

But let us be content here to define Wesley's role in a single scriptural sentence: "The kingdom of God is not meat and drink; but righteousness, and peace, and joy in the Holy Ghost" (Romans 14:17). The historic purpose of Methodism, in annotation of this text, was a plain reduction to fundamentals, a recall of a materialist and secularized generation to the essence of scriptural Christianity, a recall of the Church from her peripheral preoccupation with "meat and drink" to the heart of the Gospel, and a new definition of the cardinal terms in the Pauline vocabulary: righteousness, and peace, and joy in the Holy Ghost. "Is a man a believer in Jesus Christ and is his life suitable to his profession? are not only the *main*, but the *sole* inquiries I make in order to his admission into our Society."[1] Wesley's approach is "soteriological"; his concern is with the salvation of souls; but, as we shall come to see, his theology remains grounded in firm and strict churchmanship (*"kirchliche Dogmatik"*). There is no closer link in any other system between lecture-room, pulpit, pew, and "field"; this theology, to borrow Edwin Lewis's term, is eminently "preachable"; it administers all the necessary prophetic reminders to the traditional Church, without at any point deviating from the true apostolic tradition, and falling into the errors of sectarianism. Here is sufficient material for Methodists to engage in the study of their founder as a theologian in his own right.

From Wesley's place in theology we turn briefly to the place of theology in Wesley's system. He draws a clear distinction between doctrine and opinion which is fundamental to his thought: "You have admirably expressed," he writes to a friend,

1. *Letters*, IV.297.

"what I mean by an opinion contra-distinguished from an essential doctrine. Whatever is 'compatible with a love to Christ and a work of grace,' I term an opinion. . . . (but) right opinions are a slender part of religion, if any part of it at all."[2] There must be room for variety of opinions, as well as of theological expressions:[3] "It is the glory of the people called Methodists that they condemn none for their opinions or modes of worship. They think, and let think, and insist upon nothing but faith working by love."[4] In taking this for granted, Wesley proves himself a true son of the eighteenth century; but it never leads him to overlook or neglect, even for one moment, what the New Testament means by "sound doctrine." "Three of our travelling preachers have eagerly desired to go to America; but I could not approve of it by any means, because I am not satisfied that they thoroughly like either our discipline or our doctrine. I think they differ from our judgment in one or both."[5] It sounds antiquated to modern ears, but it is in accordance with Wesley when Synods or Conferences require their preachers to report (originally every year) that they still "believe and preach our doctrines." Without that safeguard—witness the Pastoral Epistles—the Church is unable to fulfill her obligation to preach the Gospel to every creature.

What, then, is the essence of Methodism? The Anglican heritage? William Law and the Moravians? The primitive Church and the patristic literature? The influence of the Reformers? From all these, of course, the Wesleys learnt decisively, but their theology was something at once more plain and more profound than an eclectic mixture of these various elements: "Methodism, so called, is the old religion, the religion of the Bible, the religion of the primitive Church, the religion of the Church of England" said John Wesley at the opening of the "new chapel" in City Road.[6] It is hard to recognize this "old religion" in the modern Methodism that we know; impossible to imagine that our con-

---

2. Ibid., and p. 348.
3. "Men may differ from us in their opinions, as well as their expressions, and nevertheless be partakers with us of the same precious faith." *Works*, V.238 ("Sermon on The Lord Our Righteousness").
4. *Letters*, VII.190.
5. Ibid., p. 191.
6. *Works*, VII.423.

ference agendas should find room for Wesley's invariable tripartite scheme of what to teach, how to teach, what to do; we have little time for the second item and none for the first. The Wesleyan vocabulary has been rapidly diluted and secularized; perfection tends to become complacency, fellowship mere "chumminess," and the catholic spirit indifference to any doctrinal issue. As though he had a premonition of that development, "the Reverend Mr. Wesley on being asked what should be done to keep Methodism alive after his death, returned the following answer: 'Preach our doctrine, inculcate experience, urge practice, enforce discipline. If you preach doctrine only, the people will be antinomians; if you preach experience only, they will become enthusiasts; if you preach practice only, they will become pharisees; and if you preach all these and do not enforce discipline, Methodism will be like a highly cultivated garden without a fence, posed to the ravages of the wild boar of the forest.'"[7]

"The old religion, the religion of the Bible." Methodism is synonymous with scriptural Christianity. I quote the immortal words from the preface to the *Standard Sermons:*

> To candid, reasonable men, I am not afraid to lay open what have been the inmost thoughts of my heart. I have thought, I am a creature of a day, passing through life as an arrow through the air. I am a spirit come from God, and returning to God; just hovering over the great gulf; till, a few moments hence, I am no more seen; I drop into an unchangeable eternity! I want to know one thing—the way to heaven; how to land safe on that happy shore. God Himself has condescended to teach the way; for this very end He came from heaven. He hath written it down in a book. O give me that book! At any price, give me the book of God! I have it: here is knowledge enough for me. Let me be *homo unius libri.* Here then I am, far from the busy ways of men. I sit down alone: only God is here. In His presence I open, I read His book; for this end, to find the way to heaven. . . . If any doubt still remains, I consult those who are experienced in the things of God; and then the writings whereby, being dead, they yet speak. And what I thus learn, that I teach.

---

7. I have not been able to verify this quotation which has the authentic ring of Wesley and appears under an early picture of Nicolson Square Church, Edinburgh.

16

Fundamentalism? A cheap label. Like its modernist counterpart it is really concerned with the closed Bible. Both fundamentalist and modernist have arrived at their conclusions before they ever started to open the Book.[8] Wesley cannot afford the luxury of such theories; he is too busy using the contents of scripture. In any theological argument he would be quite uninterested in his opponent's tradition or party; his sole care remains that the case should be argued biblically, and that chapter and verse should be given: "to the law and to the testimony!" (Isaiah 8:20). And he does not hesitate to bow to that judgment when it turns against himself. After his sermon on The Ministerial Office, Moore, his biographer, reports: "Wesley had encouraged me to be a man of *one book;* and he had repeatedly invited me to speak fully whatever objection I had to anything which he spoke or published. I thought that some things in that discourse were not to be found in *The Book,* and I resolved to tell him so the first opportunity. It soon occurred. . . . He looked earnestly at me for some time, but not with displeasure. He made no reply, and soon introduced another subject. I said no more. The man of *one book* could not dispute against it."[9]

There is historic significance in the reflection that Methodism was born in 1738, exactly two hundred years after England had the "open Bible" from the hands of Tyndale. The evangelical revival is nothing else but a new edition of that first "opening" of the Word to the people in their own mother tongue. Of course, "I opened my Bible" is a recurrent phrase in Wesley's writings, and one for which, time and time again, he has been taken to task. It can be abused, needless to say, but the abuse is no argument against the proper use of that particular method. "You remark," he said to one opponent, "'He applies scripture phrases to himself without attending their original meaning or once considering the difference of times and circumstances.' I answer, I am not conscious of anything like this. I apply no

8. "Distribution of Bibles without simultaneous proclamation of the Word (by living speech) is but a very inferior procedure, inadequate to the divine order which the Church must observe; it is a quasi-confidence in the magical powers of the printed book" (A.F.C. Vilmar, a Lutheran Divine of the nineteenth century, *Dogmatik,* II, 220).

9. *Works,* VII.273 (note).

scripture phrase either to myself or any other without carefully considering, both the original meaning and the secondary sense, wherein (allowing for different times and circumstances) it may be applied to ordinary Christians. . . . At some rare times, when I have been in great distress of soul, or in utter uncertainty how to act in an important case which required a speedy determination, after using all other means that occurred, I have cast lots or opened the Bible. And by this means I have been relieved from that distress or directed in that uncertainty."[10] The Confessional Church in Germany would bear witness to a similar experience in its use of the daily texts printed in the Moravian diaries, which, long before Hitler, had been in common use among Lutheran pastors and laymen. Wesley is too much at home in *The Book*, too well versed in the critical reading of the scriptures, to be touched by our modern superiority: "Upon the mention of any text, do I know the context, and the parallel places? Have I that point at least of a good Divine, the being a good textuary? Do I know the grammatical construction of the four Gospels, of the Acts, of the Epistles; and am I a master of the spiritual sense (as well as the literal) of what I read? . . . Do I understand the language of the Old Testament? Critically? At all? Can I read into English one of David's psalms, or even the first chapter of Genesis? Do I understand the language of the New Testament? Am I a critical master of it? Have I enough of it even to read into English the first chapter of St. Luke? If not, how many years did I spend at school? How many at the University? And what was I doing all those years? Ought not shame to cover my face?"[11]

Thus, in his *Address to the Clergy*, Wesley turns the criticism back upon ourselves. It has been said that Methodism as a Church is not really "Bible-conscious"; if that be true, it is our death sentence; our whole *raison d'etre* has gone. There is more at stake here than a formal principle; for the *Formalprinzip* of scripturalness, as the Lutheran fathers termed it, is inseparable from the *Materialprinzip* which is justification by Faith. This is the cardinal doctrine, discovered by the Reformers and recovered by the Wesleys, in the New Testament; and the truth of its

10. *Letters*, II.245.
11. *Works*, X.491.

content is borne out by the fact that it is found in the scriptures. "I marvelled that we were so soon and so entirely removed from Him that called us into the grace of Christ, unto another gospel. Who would believe our Church had been founded on this important article of justification by faith alone? I am astonished I should ever think this a new doctrine; especially while our Articles and Homilies stand unrepealed, and the key of knowledge is not yet taken away."[12] The note of surprise in Charles Wesley's *Journal* of May 1738 was echoed when, about forty years ago, the search for Luther's lecture notes on Romans, which had engaged libraries, seminaries and colleges all over the learned world, abruptly ended in the place from whence it had begun; a visitor to the Prussian State Library, on his way to the Reading Room, found the much-sought manuscript reposing in a glass case, ready for all to see. Which things are a parable:

> Oft I in my heart have said:
> Who shall ascend on high,
> Mount to Christ, my glorious Head,
> To bring Him from the sky?
> Borne on contemplation's wing,
> Surely I shall find Him there,
> Where the angels praise their King,
> And gain the morning star.

> Oft I in my heart have said:
> Who to the deep shall stoop,
> Sink with Christ among the dead,
> From thence to bring Him up
> Could I but my heart prepare
> By unfeigned humility,
> Christ would quickly enter there,
> And ever dwell with me.

> But the righteousness of faith
> Hath taught me better things:
> Inward turn thine eyes, it saith,
> While Christ to me it brings;
> Christ is ready to impart
> Life to all for life who sigh;

12. Charles Wesley, *Journal*, 17th May 1738.

In thy mouth and in thy heart
The word is ever nigh.[13]

It is but the same message in other words when Wesley calls it scriptural holiness; for it is the same Christ who is made unto us "righteousness and sanctification" (I Corinthians 1:30), and who "raised up His servants, John and Charles Wesley, to proclaim anew the gift of redemption and the life of holiness." The distinction in terms implies no separation in fact; for "whom He justified, them He also glorified" (Romans 8:30), and the object of God's saving grace can never be anyone or anything other than a believer. Would that later publishers of hymn-books had left us at least the precious table of contents from Wesley's early editions which makes it abundantly clear for whom he writes: "For mourners convinced of sin; for persons convinced of backslidings; for backsliders recovered; for believers rejoicing, fighting, praying, watching, working, suffering, seeking for full redemption, saved, interceding for the word, for the Society meeting, giving thanks, praying, parting."

Before looking at some of the hymns themselves, let us pause to recall the fact that Methodism, unique among the major denominations in Christendom, expresses her doctrine officially in the form of expository documents: the *Notes on the New Testament* and the *Standard Sermons.* Where others have Confessions or Articles of Faith, we (notwithstanding the twenty-five Articles) point directly to the Bible as annotated by Wesley; listening to his expert guidance, but bound only to the Word of God. In this respect the hymns, though not "official," have an authority hardly second to that of the *Notes* and *Sermons;* for what John Wesley says in footnotes on the sacred text, Charles endorses in verse (particularly in the *Hymns on Select Passages of the Holy Scriptures,* whose commentary value has yet to be discovered), and what John preaches in the form of "discourse," calls for his hearers to make response in the hymns of Charles. Others may be pitied and forgiven when the poverty of their hymn collections leaves them no choices suitable to their texts; Methodists have no excuse if they do not sing Charles Wesley or if, worse still, they mutilate his hymns. "Many Gentlemen have

13. *M.H.B.,* No. 530.

done my Brother and me (though without naming us) the honor to reprint many of our hymns. Now they are perfectly welcome so to do, provided they print them just as they are. But I desire they would not attempt to mend them—for they really are not able. None of them is able to mend either the sense or the verse. Therefore, I must beg of them one of these two favors: either to let them stand just as they are, to take them for better for worse; or to add the true reading in the margin, or at the bottom of the page; that we may no longer be accountable either for the nonsense or for the doggerel of other men."[14]

From the wealth of scriptural Christianity which is the glory of Charles Wesley's works we can only single out, in a few brief references, the hymns which deal specifically with the Bible itself.

> Come, O Thou Prophet of the Lord,
> Thou great Interpreter divine,
> Explain Thine own transmitted word,
> To teach and to inspire is Thine;
> Thou only canst Thyself reveal,
> Open the book, and loose the seal.[15]

A double inspiration is here implied: "The Spirit of God not only once inspired those who wrote it (sc. the scripture), but continually inspires, supernaturally assists, those that read it with earnest prayer."[16] The function of the "great interpreter divine" is to explain, to transmit, to teach and to inspire; and the product of the word of God so "opened" is the man of God (II Timothy 3:16–7). Another hymn, "Inspirer of the ancient seers,"[17] gives a detailed paraphrase of that passage. God's Word, said Luther, cannot be without God's people, and God's people not without God's Word.[18]

What is the content of the Bible? It is Jesus Himself, "descended from the sky," the incarnate Word, whose record is in Holy Writ:

14. John Wesley's "Preface to a collection of hymns for the use of people called Methodists," 20th October 1779.
15. *Methodist Hymn-Book* (1877), No. 90.
16. Wesley, *Notes on the New Testament;* II Timothy 3:16.
17. *Methodist Hymn-Book* (1877), No. 89.
18. Luther, *Works (Weimar Edition),* L, 629, 34.

21

Thy words are more than empty sound,
Inseparably one with Thee;
Spirit in them, and life is found,
And all the depths of Deity.[19]

It is Jesus Himself at Emmaus, opening the book that had so far been veiled and sealed, walking with His disciples, and revealing Himself to them in the breaking of bread.

O may the gracious words divine
Subject of all my converse be!
So will the Lord His follower join,
And walk and talk Himself with me;
So shall my heart His presence prove,
And burn with everlasting love.[20]

And as is shown in the same last chapter of St. Luke (24:27, 44), it is the law, the prophets and the psalms which point to Christ, crucified and risen; the hammer of God's Word (Jeremiah 23:29) which prepares the soul for the Gospel; the schoolmaster driving us, as it were, into the arms of Christ (Galatians 3:24); the mercy of God "concluding all in unbelief" (Romans 11:32). This spells the unity of Old and New Testaments in Wesley's preaching:

Come, O Thou all-victorious Lord,
Thy power to us make known;
Strike with the hammer of Thy word,
And break these hearts of stone.

Conclude us first in unbelief,
And freely then release;
Fill every soul with sacred grief,
And then with sacred peace.

Impoverish, Lord, and then relieve,
And then enrich the poor;
The knowledge of our sickness give,
The knowledge of our cure.

19. *Methodist Hymn-Book* (1877), No. 881.
20. *M.H.B.*, No. 310.

Our desperate state through sin declare,
And speak our sins forgiven;
By perfect holiness prepare,
And take us up to heaven.[21]

The word so received must be spread: "See how great a flame aspires." We shall have to return to that hymn. In other lines Wesley prays for laborers to be sent into the great harvest of his day and appeals to the great sower of the seed:

Jesu, the word bestow,
The true immortal seed;
Thy gospel then shall greatly grow,
And all our land o'erspread;

Its energy exert
In the believing soul;
Diffuse Thy grace through every part,
And sanctify the whole.[22]

Note here the twofold "penetration" which is characteristically Methodist: to every part of "our land" the Gospel must be carried, and every part of "the believing soul" ("entire sanctification") belongs to God.

About the sermons we must be even briefer. It would still be well for many of us preachers to take our founder's advice and, instead of producing—twice each Sunday!—yet more of our own, to read from time to time some of Mr. Wesley's sermons to our congregations. It would certainly be preferable to the quite unwarranted employment of sectarians and heretics in our pulpits where we cannot fill them with our own "supplies." The mere study of Wesley's titles could initiate a chapter in homiletic re-education for our age: "Awake thou that sleepest," "The Almost Christian," "The Scripture Way of Salvation," "The Righteousness of Faith," "Catholic Spirit," "A Caution against Bigotry," "The Duty of Constant Communion," "Redeeming the Time." Topical headlines? Yes, but altogether on the basis and

---

21. *M.H.B.*, No. 347. Cf. the important letter (III.78ff.) about the right method of preaching the Law and the Gospel.
22. Ibid., No. 248.

in the service of expository preaching. And in the choice of his texts, in the recurrent favorite quotations from Old and New Testaments, it is possible for us to discover the key to the whole of Wesley's theology.

For the effect of his preaching we shall, of course, have to consult the *Journal* later on. In every instance of physical weakness, preaching itself becomes the standard medicine which he prescribes for himself. At the age of eighty-seven, six months before his death, he writes: "My body seems nearly to have done its work and to be almost worn out. Last month my strength was nearly gone, and I could have sat almost still from morning to night. But, blessed be God, I crept about a little and made shift to preach once a day. On Monday I ventured a little farther; and after I had preached three times (once in the open air) I found my strength so restored that I could have preached again without inconvenience."[23] He does not leave it there; he must watch over the souls of his hearers, register their response, press unashamedly for the conversion of the individual, and gather the converts into the fellowship and under the discipline of the Methodist Society. It is plainly inconceivable that anyone could ever have got away from him with "I enjoyed you tremendously today, Mr. Wesley." Congregations are classified as either "serious" or "rude," and members meticulously examined as to "how their souls prosper." This is indeed "preaching for a verdict," yet not for a quick and cheap emotional "decision," but for the lasting commitment expressed in the solemn Covenant Service to which the Methodist people were recalled year by year, so that their backslidings should be freely healed by the restoring power of the living Word.

Archbishop Secker had a simple way of explaining Wesley's great success; he called him a "dispenser of physic who dances on a slack-rope," and ascribed the mass-attendances at his early services to "the sheer novelty and irregularity of his methods."[24] We prefer to accept Wesley's own estimate: "If I have been indeed advancing nothing but the true knowledge and love of God, if God has made me an instrument in reforming many sinners and bringing them to inward and pure religion,

---

23. *Letters*, VIII.237–8.
24. John S. Simon, *John Wesley and the Methodist Societies*, p. 279.

and if many of these continue holy until this day and free from all wilfull sin, then may I, even I, use those awful words: 'He that despiseth me, despiseth Him that sent me.' But I never expect the world to allow me one of these points. However, I must go on as God shall enable me; I must lay out whatsoever He entrusts me with in advancing the true Christian knowledge of God and the love and fear of God among men, in reforming those that are yet without God in the world, in propagating inward and pure religion, righteousness, peace, and joy in the Holy Ghost."[25]

After the Hymns and *Sermons*, last but not least, the *Notes*—that is, Johann Albrecht Bengel's *Gnomon Novi Testamenti*, which Wesley esteemed so highly that he preferred to translate and shorten it for the good of the Methodist people rather than to attempt a commentary of his own. In contemporary Germany [of the 1950s] Bengel is just beginning to come into his own again; maybe from there Methodism will be brought to a new appreciation of this much-neglected and much-maligned standard book of our doctrine. Let Bengel speak for himself: "The *Gnomon* must be supposed to say: 'The text runs thus, not otherwise. This, and no other, is the noun; this, the verb; this, the particle; this, the case; this, the tense; this is the arrangement of the words; this is the repetition or interchange of words; this, the succession of arguments; this, the emotion of the mind, etc.' . . . It is not our part arrogantly to define, but humbly to believe what is worthy of God (I Corinthians 2:1, 14:21)."[26] This effectively disposes of the modern brand of commentator who with utter certainty lays down the law as to what St. Paul "could" or "could not" have written. Bengel, and Wesley with him, is concerned solely to listen to the voice of God in the Word: "Speak, Lord, thy servant heareth." "I have long since given the name of Gnomon, a modest, and, I think, appropriate title, to these exegetical annotations, which perform the office of an index; it is, in short, my intention, briefly to point out, or indicate, the full force of words and sentences in the New Testament, so that the reader, being introduced by the straight road into the text, may find as rich pasture there

25. *Letters*, II.273.
26. Bengel, *Gnomon Novi Testamenti*, I.50 (Fausset's English translation).

25

as possible. The *Gnomon* points the way with sufficient clearness. If you are wise, the text itself teaches you all things."[27] But something more is needed than intellectual and devotional equipment. When Wesley comes, in the fifth chapter of Revelation, to the passage where John "wept much, because no man was found worthy to open and to read the book," he notes: "The Revelation was not written without tears; neither without tears will it be understood."[28] Here is an echo of Luther's famous translation of Isaiah 28:19: "Temptation makes us listen to the Word." Like him, and like Bengel, Wesley knew what it was to be trained in the threefold school of *oratio-meditatio-tentatio.*

And like the Lutheran fathers, he found the characteristic marks of scripture in its authority, perspicuity, sufficiency, and efficacy. "By far the more numerous portions of the sacred text (thanks be to God)," writes Bengel—and he had produced his own critical apparatus—"labour under no variety deserving notice. These portions contain the whole scheme of salvation, and establish every particular of it by every test of truth. Every various reading ought and may be referred to these portions, and decided by them as by a normal standard."[29] "Scripture," echoes Wesley, "interprets scripture; one part fixing the sense of another. . . . It is certain none can be a good Divine who is not a good textuary."[30] Attention to the individual passage or even to the context is not enough in itself; it is really a *system* of notes on the New Testament which Bengel's *Gnomon* represents, and there is no reason at all to be ashamed or nervous of the use of that word. The future systematic theology of Methodism could well be such a system of notes on the sacred text. For "the holy men of God, both in the Old and in the New Testament, exhibit, not only an exact knowledge of the Truth, but also a systematic arrangement of their subject, a precise expression of their meaning, and a genuine strength of feeling. . . . In the works of God, even to the smallest plant, there is the most entire symmetry; in the words of God there is

27. Ibid.
28. Wesley, *Notes on the New Testament* (Revelation 5:4).
29. Bengel, *Gnomon*, I.13.
30. *Works*, X.482.

the most systematic perfection, even to a letter."[31] No one will pretend that Bengel said the last word about this; no one will deny that his formalistic tendency could, and did on occasions, carry him to extremes. Still, even in the last book of the Bible, where the *Notes* are most notoriously at fault, where the beasts are taken to represent the several Popes and the millennium to begin in 1836—even there are hidden treasures which Methodist preachers today ignore to their loss. Let one illustration suffice. The song of the four living creatures in Revelation 4:8 is, naturally, linked to Isaiah 6:3, and after a full analysis of the biblical meaning of "holy," Wesley's *Note* goes on: "This holiness is often styled glory; often His holiness and glory are celebrated together. For holiness is covered glory, and glory is uncovered holiness." Do you feel you want to read another commentary when you have read this?

Take the Epistle to the Romans which, after all, was the gate through which Wesley entered into the understanding of the saving faith, and observe how the whole function of his theology is, as it were, to annotate the text by underlining certain thoughts and phrases in each chapter: 1:16–17, "The just shall live by faith"—the cardinal doctrine of justification; 2:29, "Circumcision is that of the heart, in the spirit and not in the letter"—the theme of Wesley's great sermon and the basis for his distinction between the true and the false Church; 3:31, "The law established by faith"—another standard sermon, defending the Reformation safeguard against the abuses of Antinomianism; 5:5, "The love of God is shed abroad in our hearts by the Holy Ghost"—Pentecost illustrated in the Aldersgate experience; 7:24, "Who shall deliver me from the body of this death?"—the believer seeking for full redemption, and the sweet singer of Methodism longing to "shout our great deliverer's praise"; 8:16, "The Spirit beareth witness with our spirit"—the answer to the cry of Chapter 7 in the twofold witness of assurance, and the move, in the same context, from "bondage" to "adoption"; 10:6–8, "the word is nigh thee"—the search of the Oxford days, heaven of speculation or abyss of mystical experience, is ended through the revelation of the

31. Bengel, *Gnomon*, I.42–3.

nearby Christ in the written and preached word; 10:14–15, "How shall they hear without a preacher, how shall they preach, except they be sent?"—the latent prayer of eighteenth-century England answered in the raising of the Wesleys by God Himself, and the warrant for the evangelical mission of Methodism;[32] 11:22, "If thou continue in his goodness; otherwise thou also shalt be cut off"—Wesley's fight against the Calvinist notion of the "final perseverance of the saints," and his insistence upon the daily need of applying Christ's merit; 11:32, "Concluded them all in unbelief, that He might have mercy upon all"—the other side of the Calvinist controversy: Christ died for all; 12:1, "That ye present your bodies a living sacrifice"—the response to Christ's self-offering in the Eucharistic hymns of Charles Wesley; 13:8, "Owe no man anything, but to love one another"—the self-giving, introduced in the previous passage, culminates in the doctrine of perfect love; 14:1, 15:1, "We that are strong ought to bear the infirmities of the weak"—the Magna Carta of tolerance in Methodism, and the still needed "caution against bigotry"; 15:18–21, "Nothing which Christ hath not wrought by me . . . not where Christ was named . . . I have fully preached the gospel"—there is, in a nutshell, Wesley's doctrine of the ministry which takes its authority directly from the living Christ, addresses its commission specifically to "those who are without," and glories in the *plerophoria*, the fullness of the blessing of the Gospel (verse 29).

Fullness, to use this concluding phrase, is the hallmark of Wesley's scriptural Christianity, and it is this for which Methodism stands—not for any petty doctrines, any new invention, any singling-out of favorite notions from the economy of the New Testament. Someone challenged Wesley that "singularities are your most beloved opinions and favourite tenets, more insisted upon by you than the general and uncontroverted truths of Christianity"; he answers: "And so, I doubt, it will be to the end of the world; for, in spite of all I can say, they will represent one circumstance of my doctrine (so called) as the main substance of it. . . . 'No singularities' is not my answer; but that no singularities are my most beloved opinions; that no singular-

32. *Journal,* 25th May 1765.

ities are more, or near as much, insisted upon by me as the general, uncontroverted truths of Christianity."[33] Both pre- and post-Wesleyan theologies have fallen far short of what Wesley set out to discover. Even the Reformers were inclined to be content with the "givenness" of the scriptural canon, the historic fulfilment of which our Lord speaks in His first sermon at Nazareth (Luke 4:21) and to overlook the even greater promise of "fullness" of truth and joy into which, according to John 16:13, 24, the Paraclete will guide the disciples. Similarly, contemporary thought and energy seem to be absorbed in the historic analysis of "Christ and Time" and strangely oblivious of that succession by which the third article of the Creed follows upon the second. Despite our alleged and repeated insistence upon the "concrete here and now" of the revelation, our language becomes markedly abstract and halting when (if!) we try to speak about the Holy Ghost. "Luther says: 'The little word *Father*, said formally, i.e. without meaning, in the heart is eloquence superior to what Demosthenes and Cicero could deliver.' What reason had Luther for making such a daring statement? The only one: viz., that he knew the case of divine seriousness, in which a man, in his extreme weakness and badness, not in an experience of religious profundity, but laid hold of in that sighing which had become utterly unimportant in his religiosity, had become born as God's child, because it had pleased God to take this groaning, sighing man, together with his burden, upon Himself. This grave circumstance is the presence of the Spirit of Promise."[34]

No, he would be a bold man (even if he were Karl Barth himself, who wrote these words in the 1930s) who would persuade us to recognize St. Paul or St. John in this guise. "Lo, now speakest Thou plainly, and speakest no proverb" (John 16:29; II Corinthians 3:12ff.)—that is the authentic note of Pentecost. No qualification, no conjunctive, no dialectic; but the plain, cat-

33. The Bishop of Bristol to Wesley: "If you preach, it must be according to the order; the order of the Church of England upon ordination." Wesley: "What does your Lordship mean by ordination?" Bishop: "Do not you know what I mean?" Wesley: "If you mean that sending spoken of in Romans 10, I had it." Bishop: "I mean that. What mission had you?" Wesley: "I had a mission from God and man" (*Journal*, 25th May 1765).

34. Karl Barth, *The Holy Ghost and The Christian Life* (1938), p. 86.

egorical declaration: "The Spirit beareth witness with our spirit, that we are the children of God." Again, no hypothetical "blessing" in the narrow, technical, sectarian sense of that phrase to which we shall have to return, but the real presence of the living Christ through His Spirit in the believer and in the Church. "For our gospel came not unto you in word only, but also in power, and in the Holy Ghost, and in much assurance" (I Thessalonians 1:5). So it is the Word which mediates the Spirit, and the Spirit which opens the Word; so the persistent "now, now" of Charles Wesley is vindicated, and the way is prepared for that doctrine of the Holy Spirit which Methodist theology has yet to offer in answer to the general need of Christ's Church today.

There is no time left for me to develop this theme by a reference to the presence and function of the Paraclete in Wesley's hymns, which contain a wealth of material for the construction of a scriptural Pneumatology. All I can do is to sum up in one sentence the meaning of scriptural Christianity according to the Wesleys: it is the Gospel, the whole Gospel, and nothing but the Gospel; it is the fullness of Him in whom all the promises of God are Yea and Amen (II Corinthians 1:20) and in whom—see the Christmas hymns—the "fullness of Deity" dwells bodily (Colossians 2:9), who imparts His Spirit to His people, leading them beyond the crisis-religion of John the Baptist into the perfect daylight of "the bright and morning star" (Revelation 22:16), so that the believers in turn are, as in the New Testament, full of grace and truth, full of good works, full of joy, and full of the Holy Ghost.

> Give me the enlarged desire,
> And open, Lord, my soul,
> Thine own fullness to require,
> And comprehend the whole:
> Stretch my faith's capacity
> Wider, and yet wider still;
> Then with all that is in Thee
> My soul for ever fill![35]

35. *M.H.B*, No. 31.

2

Practical

The meaning of "practice" for Wesley is precisely parallel to the
meaning of scriptural Christianity. Practice is simply and
plainly enforcement of Christianity. As Methodism, in the first
definition, was "the old Bible religion, the religion of the primitive Church and of the Church of England," with the one important difference that the Wesleys meant to keep that religion
and put it into action, so practical Christianity seizes upon the
promise in Jeremiah 31 and parallel passages, where again the
whole distinction between the old and the new covenants can be
summed up in the statement that henceforth people shall keep
God's word, walk in His judgments and have His law written in
their hearts. There is nothing new here in content; only the
stony tables are replaced by the "fleshy tables of the heart"
(II Corinthians 3:3). The practical Christianity of John and
Charles Wesley is what the Pietists of the previous generation
called the *praxis pietatis,* or, in a much earlier phrase, the practice of the presence of God. In other words, it is the practice of
prayer—from which, for Wesley, all other Christian activities
are inseparable. Prayer lays hold upon the promise of Pentecost, with which we concluded the first chapter, and claims the
gift of the Spirit for God's people here and now:

> Father, if justly still we claim
> To us and ours the promise made,
> To us be graciously the same,
> And crown with living fire our head.
>
> Our claim admit, and from above
> Of holiness the Spirit shower,

Of wise discernment, humble love,
And zeal, and unity, and power.

The Spirit of faith, in this Thy day,
To break the power of cancelled sin,
Tread down its strength, o'erturn its sway,
And still the conquest more than win.

The Spirit breathe of inward life,
Which in our hearts Thy laws may write;
Then grief expires, and pain, and strife;
'Tis nature all, and all delight.[1]

That unity of devotion and service can again be concisely expressed in two single lines of well-known hymns: "To serve my God alone" and "To serve the present age."[2] It is unity reflecting the rhythm in the life of our Lord "'twixt the mount and multitude" which Wesley describes elsewhere,[3] between "departing into a solitary place" and "going into the next town" (Mark 1:35–8). Let me be content with a brief note on each of these two aspects. First, when we speak of worship as the service of God, we are bound to remember that Wesley gave us—and to American Methodists in particular—a definite form and order. "I have prepared a Liturgy little differing from that of the Church of England (I think, the best constituted national Church in the world) which I advise all the travelling preachers to use on the Lord's Day in all the congregations, reading the Litany only on Wednesdays and Fridays and praying extempore on all other days. I also advise the elders to administer the Supper of the Lord on every Lord's Day."[4] That, be it noted, is Methodism! "Undoubtedly," says a modern observer, "Wesley organized his people on the basis of a sacramental society. . . . His ideal was that the Lord's Supper should be administered on every Lord's Day. As far as possible, this was the constant practice in the earliest Methodist chapels. The Sunday-morning service normally consisted of the preaching of the Word and the administration

1. *M.H.B.*, No. 284.
2. Ibid., Nos. 594 and 578.
3. Ibid., No. 598, "Holy Lamb, who Thee confess."
4. *Letters*, VII.239.

32

of the Lord's Supper—a perfect synthesis of evangelical and sacramental fellowship."[5] To which we must add the reminder that Wesley produced forms of prayer for regular use, prayers for families, for children, for every morning and evening of the week; and the recent edition by Frederick C. Gill has proved that they can still be used to the advantage of the Methodist people.[6] Wesley knew and taught us that God is not the author of confusion, but of order.

As there is form of devotion, so there is form of practical service, and it is laid down by Wesley in the Rules and in the Plan. To the latter, the itinerant system which characterizes Methodism in distinction from other Churches, we shall have to return in the next chapter; to the Rules, Henry Carter has given us an invaluable guide in *The Methodist—A Survey of the Christian "Way,"* which is still as readable and applicable as it was at its first publication in 1914.[7] Doing no harm, doing good, attending upon all the ordinances of God—these are sound, indeed pedestrian and elementary, principles for members of the Christian Church. That they do not go without saying, and are not yet out of date, has been brought home to us by the voice of an outsider: Victor Gollancz in his book *Our Threatened Values.* What he predicted in 1946 has been pathetically justified by the events of the intervening years, and we in the Churches may well be humbled by the reflection that it was a Jew who spoke when most of us were silent.[8] The flood which threatens our values and which it is our duty to stem is, in Gollancz's words, "contempt for pity, self-righteousness, attacks on freedom of speech, decay of intellectual integrity, normalization of resistance traits, nationalism and racialism, barbaric 'justice'"; and it is highly significant to hear from a passionate socialist that "the essential battle today is not between capitalism and mere socialism as such, but between the liberal or Christian ethic, of which humanistic socialism is the crown, and totalitarianism in

5. T. H. Barratt, in *Methodism, Its Present Responsibilities*, Bristol Congress (1929), p. 68.

6. Frederick C. Gill, ed., *John Wesley's Prayers* (London: Epworth Press, 1951).

7. Henry Carter, *Methodist—A Survey of the Christian "Way."*

8. Victor Gollancz, *Our Threatened Values* (London, 1946).

all its forms."[9] Of course, I am not pretending that this is Methodism; but I am positive that it is at least "note and comment" to which Wesley would subscribe today. For a good deal of what he has to say about practical Christianity calls for, and has acted as, a barrier in defence of "our threatened values"; and it implies, at the same time, the breaking down of all false and selfish barriers—between classes, races, nations, and parties—which men have erected to bar each other's way into the Kingdom of God.

J. Ernest Rattenbury has described this side of Wesley as "a religion of common sense." It is the legacy of the eighteenth century, and it is still precious at such a time as this. Of course, Wesley had his own brand of "rationalism." He would, with all the reason at his command, "appeal to all men of reason and religion"; he would stand no Deism, no nonsense, and no "dialectic" theology of the twentieth-century type. His reaction to Jacob Böhme is typical: "It strikes at the root of all revealed religion, by making men think meanly of the Bible; a natural effect of thinking Behmen more highly illuminated than any or all of the Apostles. So Mr. S. frankly acknowledged: 'While I admired him, I thought St. Paul and St. John very mean writers.' Indeed it quite spoils the taste for plain, simple religion, such as the Bible is; and gives a false taste, which can relish nothing so well, as high, obscure, unintelligible jargon."[10]

It would be tempting to speculate about Wesley's role as a critic of contemporary theology in the light of these words; but we must pass on to something more constructive. What is the practical meaning of Methodism? Whenever he sets out to answer this question, we observe that the focus is on the person of the Christian: thus he writes about the character of a Methodist, the principles of a Methodist, the history of the people called Methodists. Incidentally, he writes in beautiful plain English, "for plain, unlettered men, who understand only their mother-tongue, and yet reverence and love the Word of God, and have a desire to save their souls,"[11] and in the form of cheap brief

9. Ibid., p. 156.
10. *Works*, IX.514. Cf. *Letters*, II.317: "Who can believe both the sides of a contradiction?" and the dispute with Zinzendorf (*Works*, X.203, 6).
11. Preface to Wesley, *Notes on the New Testament*.

tracts, which in recent reprints have gone far to prove that John Wesley still sells very much better than our experts would have us believe. "Christianity . . . is that system of doctrine which describes the character above recited, which promises it shall be mine (provided I will not rest till I attain), and which tells me how I may attain it."[12]

Lest, therefore, theology should lose sight of the Christian man with whom it has to deal, we ask: "'What then is the mark? Who is a Methodist, according to your own account?' I answer: A Methodist is one who has 'the love of God shed abroad in his heart by the Holy Ghost given unto him'; one who 'loves the Lord his God with all his heart, and with all his soul, and with all his mind, and with all his strength.' God is the joy of his heart, and the desire of his soul; which is constantly crying out, 'Whom have I in heaven but thee?' . . . These are the principles and practices of our sect; these are the marks of a true Methodist. By these alone do those who are in derision so called, desire to be distinguished from other men. If any man say: 'Why, these are only the common, fundamental principles of Christianity!' thou hast said; so I mean; this is the very truth; I know they are no other; and I would to God both thou and all men knew, that I, and all who follow my judgment, do vehemently refuse to be distinguished from other men, by any but the common principles of Christianity—the plain, old Christianity that I teach, renouncing and detesting all other marks of distinction."[13]

The Methodist is not distinct from other men. Yes, but he is very distinct, as Wesley points out in the same passage, from all formal, nominal, ornamental and conventional Christians. How else could he preach on the marks of the new birth, on the great privilege of those born of God? There is, after all, that sequence of sentences in the *First Epistle of St. John*, all of which begin: "Hereby we know . . ."—"Hereby we know that we are of the truth" (3:19); "Hereby we know that he abideth in us" (3:24); "Hereby we know that we dwell in him" (4:13); "Hereby we know that we love the children of God" (5:2); "Hereby know ye the Spirit of God" (4:2). Wesley's picture of the Methodist is definite, and his vision of "perfect love" undoubtedly johannine. It

12. *Letters*, II.380.
13. *Works*, VIII.341, 346.

35

is something great and vital for us to recover; but also something to be purified and broadened beyond the limits of his conception. For his picture is not final, and his vision not unblurred; in certain details, a streak of narrow Puritanism has to be admitted, which leads him to reduce the fullness of Christ, of which we spoke, more nearly to the "bareness" of the Gospel. Take, for an illustration, the sermon, "In what sense we are to leave the world," with his piece of advice to parents: "Parents are almost as nearly connected with their children [sc. as husband and wife]. You cannot part with them while they are young; it being your duty to 'train them up,' with all care, 'in the way wherein they should go.' How frequently you should converse with them when they are grown up is to be determined by Christian prudence. . . . As for all other relatives, even brothers or sisters, if they are of the world, you are under no obligation to be intimate with them; you may be civil and friendly at a distance."[14] Viewed in the light of Wesley's whole theology, this is a detail which might be ignored (or which, in a given exceptional situation, might even be scripturally defended); but turned into an independent principle of interpretation and conduct, it cannot fail to distort the meaning of Methodism beyond all proportion. This is not so rare and remote a possibility as it may sound; it is, on the contrary, symptomatic of certain current and recurrent misconceptions of Methodism to which we must turn our attention now. The first of these is that a Methodist is distinct by the things which he must not do. A Methodist in Germany may drink, but must not smoke. A Methodist in Britain may smoke, but must not drink. A Methodist in America, so far as I know, must neither drink nor smoke. It is a list of taboos that evidently varies from one country to the next and from one generation to another. I have not, at this moment of writing, the answer I sought from an expert to the question of a Drew student: "Did Wesley ever drink beer?" But I do remember that a number of brewers figure in his early lists of society members at Bristol, and that, on the other hand, "green tea" was the poison against which he warned his countrymen. Am I wrong in the assumption that, if Wesley were to speak to us about this

14. *Works*, VI.462.

issue today, he would have us put first things first, remind us that, for example, war is a greater enemy than drink, and that in our public witness and crusades a revision of our priorities is long overdue? This is one of the fields where the instinctive re-action of the world to the failure of the Church could teach us that the children of darkness are in their generation wiser than the children of light.

Methodism is not, in the wording of Colossians 2:21, a reli-gion of "touch not, taste not, handle not"; the "seventy years of legal night," of which the Wesleys spoke when looking back upon their mother's life, have once and for all been left behind in their evangelical conversion. And that implies the condemna-tion of the second error: the belief that a Methodist is distinct by the things which he must do. Here again the list of objectives varies according to time, place, and circumstance. If in Wesley's day Moravian Quietism made him insist upon the necessity of good works, in our age it is Methodist Activism which would make him vote against us in defence of the freedom of the Gos-pel. Efforts, targets, statistics—how many of our Churches on both sides of the Atlantic manage to exhaust their whole life in one interminable chain of all these! It is sobering to hear the voice of Wesley on Church membership: "I inquired into the state of the Society. Most pompous accounts had been sent to me, from time to time, of the great numbers that were added to it; so that I confidently expected to find therein 6–700 members. And how is the real fact? I left 394 members, and I doubt if there are now 396! Let this be a warning to us all how we give in to that hateful custom of painting things beyond the life. Let us make a conscience of magnifying or exaggerating anything. Let us rather speak under than above the truth. We, of all men, should be punctual in all we say, that none of our words fall to the ground."[15] The work of God, be it remembered, which was the subject of all the "several conversations between the Revd Mr Wesley and others' at their early Conferences, was never pri-marily our work for God, let alone a glorification of any human program or achievement in the service of the kingdom (our per-petual "votes of thanks" would have been as unthinkable for

15. *Journal*, 16th March 1748.

him as they were in the councils of the Apostles); it was always the work which God had wrought in the souls of the people and in the midst of His Church. The very word "business" has a strange solemn meaning for Wesley: "'Tis all my business here, Lamb!" [16] The servant of the Lord, the laborer in God's harvest is with him, as with Luther, "a restless spirit enjoying the highest rest,"[17] because, justified by faith, he knows that the height of activity is reached when we let God "take over" and do His work in us (John 6:29):

> Behold the servant of the Lord!
> I wait Thy guiding eye to feel,
> To hear and keep Thy every word,
> To prove and do Thy perfect will,
> Joyful from my own works to cease,
> Glad to fulfill all righteousness.[18]

The third and last error is more subtle and grave than the others; it is the notion that a Methodist is distinct by a certain "something" he must have, commonly called his "experience." This is what so shrewd an observer as Monsignor Ronald Knox, in his chapter on Wesley, has to say about our "enthusiasm": "At the heart of him, the Evangelical is always an experimentalist. He feels certain that something has happened to him, and he invites you to let it happen to you—that is, really, the whole of his message. And if he is in a position to assure you that when this experience of conversion befell him it took six strong men to hold him down, you will be less likely (he argues) to suspect that it was just your fancy. . . . Where it [sc. the Evangelical movement] failed was in its long-term effects. Religion became identified in the popular mind with a series of moods, in which the worshipper, disposed thereto by all the arts of the revivalist, relished the flavors of spiritual peace. You needed neither a theol-

16. *M.H.B.*, No. 874 (the Wesley's Birthday Hymn), verses 5–6.
17. Luther, *Works (Weimar Edition,)* XLV.540; Ibid., VI.247, 26ff, where Luther interprets the hallowing of the Sabbathman's cessation (enforced by suffering) from his own works to the end that God alone should dwell and work in him.
18. *M.H.B.*, No. 572. The hymn is an intergral part of the Ordination Service in the British Conference's *Book of Offices*.

ogy nor a liturgy; you did not take the strain of intellectual inquiry, nor associate yourself whole-heartedly with any historic tradition of worship."[19] A complete caricature of Wesley, of course; but one which could not have been quite so firmly established without the connivance and even the encouragement of forces in our own ranks. When Dietrich Bonhoeffer in his posthumous *Ethik*[20] speaks of "Methodism," it is the same phenomenon, and not the authentic version, to which his criticism is relevant: the identification of "religion"—a word he is determined to abolish—with "a series of moods," the attempt to prepare for salvation by "Christian endeavour" in a self-appointed "method" of conversion, the artificial turning of men into the "religious type" of sinners who, by working out or being worked up into a "Damascus experience," can assure themselves of the saving grace. Faith thus becomes an effort, and experience a work by which we are justified. But when Bonhoeffer goes on to contrast and replace this kind of "method" by what he calls *Weg-bereitung*—that is, the scriptural notion of preparing the way for Him who is always there before us (John 1:30), marching into territory already conquered by the "captain of our salvation" (Hebrews 2:8–10)—he finds himself, unknowingly, entirely at one with Wesley:

> At last I own it cannot be
> That I should fit myself for Thee:
> Here then to Thee I all resign;
> Thine is the work, and only Thine.
>
> The mansion for Thyself prepare,
> Dispose my heart by entering there;
> 'Tis this alone can make me clean,
> 'Tis this alone can cast out sin.[21]

This is the end of "Methodism"; it is the beginning of Aldersgate; in other words, it is the Scripture Way of Salvation. There is no room for any attempt to copy "Damascus" in our own lives or to reproduce, in a compulsory scheme, the pre-conversion

19. Knox, (Oxford, 1950), pp. 588–9.
20. Bonhoeffer, *Ethik*.
21. *M.H.B.*, No. 344. cf. *Poetical Works*, X.96 (on Micah 2:7).

experience of the Wesleys. On the contrary: "We desire not that others should wander out of the way as we have done before them; but rather that they may profit by our loss, that they may go (though we did not, having then no man to guide us) the straight way to the religion of love, even by faith."[22] Similarly Bengel: "We should fare badly, if, in order to ascertain the royal road of truth it were necessary for us to obtain an accurate knowledge, and make a personal survey, of all the tracks which lead away from it."[23] No saner advice was ever given than that which Wesley received from Peter Böhler: "Preach the faith until thou hast it, and then preach it, because thou hast it"; any other "method" can lead only to despair. The same tolerance, therefore, that we have seen Wesley apply to opinions and expressions, must be extended to emotions, lest Methodists should forever be lost in having to conform to Ronald Knox's description.

If this is all that Methodism is not, what then is it? "This is the victory . . . that faith, which is not only an unshaken assent to all that God hath revealed in Scripture but . . . likewise the revelation of Christ in our hearts; a divine evidence or conviction of His love, His free, unmerited love to me a sinner, a sure confidence in His pardoning mercy, wrought in us by the Holy Ghost; a confidence whereby every true believer is enabled to bear witness, I know that my Redeemer liveth, I have an Advocate with the Father, Jesus Christ the righteous is my Lord, and the propitiation for my sins; I know that He hath loved me, and given Himself for me, He hath reconciled me, even me, to God; and I have redemption through His blood, even the forgiveness of sins."[24] There is evidently positive experience here and a proper place for emotion. But it is not that peculiar "something" which one type of Christian can boast against the others; it is not the thoroughly unscriptural and unattractive "second blessing," which is but the poorer Protestant edition of the Romanist *gratia infusa;* least of all has it any connexion with the tritheistic heresy that would grade us all in successive stages according to our separable accounts of Father, Son and Holy Ghost in our

22. *Works,* VIII.4.
23. Bengel, *Gnomon,* I.51.
24. *Works,* V.205.

lives. No, Wesley's "heart religion" demands and claims the dwelling of the triune God Himself in His human temple; and all the growth in knowledge, experience and holiness is for ever a growth *in Christ*. As the Lutheran fathers put it; it is God Himself, not the gifts of God, making His habitation in the believers,[25] and the "object of my first desire" is nothing and nobody else but the living Christ who is the end of the law and of all "method," and the author and finisher of our faith.[26] He "giveth not the Spirit by measure" (John 3:34); His grace can neither be manipulated nor monopolized; it is, in the words of Wesley's sermon, free in all and free for all, and to claim and take it, share it and "humbly ask for more"[27] is the evangelical form of practical Christianity.

But as concerning the social Gospel, brethren, ye need not that I teach you; for you in America have learned it much better than we in other parts of Christendom. Only let me draw your attention to the theological motivation of Wesley's vast social program. It can again be read in the choice of the texts which he employs in this connection; "heart religion" means, of course, that "whatsoever ye do, do it heartily, as to the Lord, and not unto men" (Colossians 3:23), and living faith is that "which worketh by love" (Galatians 5:6). The decisive factor in the picture with which we began this chapter and to which we have just now been led back, is once more the gift of the Holy Spirit. Note, in the following hymn, how from this starting-point we arrive, by natural transition, at the concrete details of practical Christianity:

> Jesus, the gift divine I know,
> The gift divine I ask of Thee;
> That living water now bestow,
> Thy Spirit and Thyself, on me;
> Thou, Lord, of life the Fountain art;
> Now let me find Thee in my heart.
>
> Thee let me drink, and thirst no more
> For drops of finite happiness;

25. *Formula Concordiae*, Part I, Art. III. §6; cf. John 14:23.
26. Toplady's hymn: "Object of my first desire," *M.H.B*, No. 90.
27. cf. *M.H.B.*, Nos. 399 and 383: "The sole return Thy love requires is that we ask for more."

Spring up, O well, in heavenly power,
In streams of pure perennial peace,
In joy that none can take away,
In life which shall for ever stay.

Father, on me the grace bestow,
Unblamable before Thy sight,
Whence all the streams of mercy flow;
Mercy, Thy own supreme delight,
To me, for Jesu's sake, impart,
And plant Thy nature in my heart.

Thy mind throughout my life be shown,
While, listening to the sufferer's cry,
The widow's and the orphan's groan,
On mercy's wings I swiftly fly,
The poor and helpless to relieve,
My life, my all, for them to give.

Thus may I show the Spirit within,
Which purges me from every stain;
Unspotted from the world and sin,
My faith's integrity maintain;
The truth of my religion prove
By perfect purity and love.[28]

"On mercy's wings I swiftly fly"—it is important to catch the
note of urgency here. The King's business requires haste: "Who
knows what a year may bring forth? It may carry both me and
you into a better world! Therefore let us live today!"[29] The last
hour is always on Wesley's mind, as he goes about his "business"; at fifty, in a critical illness, he has his epitaph prepared:
"In the evening (not knowing how it might please God to dis-
pose of me), to prevent vile panegyric, I wrote as follows: 'Here
lieth the body of John Wesley, a brand plucked out of the burn-
ing, who died of a consumption in the fifty-first year of his age,
not leaving, after his debts are paid, ten pounds behind him;
praying, God be merciful to me, an unprofitable servant.'"[30]

28. *M.H.B.*, No. 605.
29. *Letters*, VIII.228.
30. *Journal*, 26th November 1753.

When he goes to Bedford to preach to the assembled judges, "The Great Assize" is his theme, and "we shall all stand before the judgment seat of Christ" (Romans 14:10) his text; when he gathers the newly-won members into the Methodist Society, the sole test of admission is "the desire to be saved from their sins and to flee from the wrath to come." Thus he revives the Reformers' *theologia viatoris* and sharpens their emphasis on "redeeming the time"; and his sense of stewardship, of the "strict account," leads him to economize in the discussion of theological issues and to weigh the merely academic and partisan against that which will ultimately count in the day of the Lord Jesus Christ. "It has long been my rule," wrote Bengel, "to write no word of which I might repent in my last hour."[31] Romans 9:28 is one of Wesley's great favorites: "He will finish the work, and cut it short in righteousness; because a short work will the Lord make upon the earth"; and it is significant that this was also the text of Asbury's last sermon.

Here is the characteristic voice of Methodism that one would wish to hear with far greater emphasis in the chorus of the Churches at Evanston—neither the apocalyptic futurism of the East, nor the humanistic optimism of the West, but the genuine hope of the New Testament: "Thanks be to God, which giveth us the victory through our Lord Jesus Christ. Therefore, my beloved brethren, be ye steadfast, unmovable, always abounding in the work of the Lord, forasmuch as ye know that your labor is not in vain in the Lord" (I Corinthians 15:57–8). In his inaugural address as Dean of Drew Theological Seminary, Clarence Tucker Craig gave us this timely reminder about the "Methodist emphasis in theological education": "When books now appear from the pen of those who led this revolution in Christian thinking, they contain little but stale repetition about the ambiguities of our human situation, and further analyses of the involvement of men in a sinful society. Reading these, one is inevitably led to the impression that the final word of our religion must be: 'Who shall deliver me from the body of this death?' I do not want to caricature the helpful work of any great thinker. But I do think it is high time for the Christian Church to answer this pivotal

31. Oscar Wächter, *Johann Albrecht Bengel* (1865), p. 70.

question: Does our faith offer men simply a truer insight into the human predicament, or does it offer a realizable redemption to those who live amid this predicament? There can be no doubt about the New Testament position. Here stands the confident assurance that in Christ God has reconciled men to Himself, so that peace is now possible, even though there are limitations of human experience not yet removed. Do we no longer believe this, or is it the obligation of those who inherit the Methodist tradition to lift up by word and deed this truth which is so badly needed today? An emphasis upon the reality of the redeemed life should be central in any Methodist seminary."[32]

"They are saved by hope," said Wesley of the Christians, "by this hope of a total change with a gradually increasing salvation."[33] "The world passeth away, and the lust thereof: but he that doeth the will of God abideth for ever" (I John 2:17). We end where we began: what is the "thing" that wants "doing" in the practical Christianity of the Wesleys? It is nothing else but the Word of God, the word which Jesus preached and which He commanded, at the end of the Sermon on the Mount, to be heard and done. Hearing and doing are one thing; the foolish man who doeth not, only shows that he has never heard. St. James (1:22ff) confirms St. Matthew, and, according to Wesley's Notes,[34] also St. Paul; for "the general rule of interpreting Scripture is this: the literal sense of every text is to be taken, if it be not contrary to some other texts; but in that case the obscure text is to be interpreted by those which speak more plainly."[35] This unity exists not only within the New Testament, but also between the Old and the New; the will of God in the old covenant is now, as we have seen, "written in our hearts," so that the believer's "delight is in the law of the Lord" (Psalm 1:2).

32. *Drew University Bulletin* (1949).
33. *Works*, VIII.329.
34. "And yet there is no contradiction between the apostles: because (1) they do not speak of the same faith; St. Paul speaking of living faith; St. James here, of dead faith; (2) they do not speak of the same works: St. Paul speaking of works antecedent to faith; St. James of works subsequent to it" (Wesley, *Notes on the New Testament*, James 2:24). One wonders whether Wesley would qualify for Luther's offer of his doctor's beret to the man who could reconcile St. James with St. Paul!
35. *Letters*, III.129.

And yet the glory of the new dispensation exceeds and super-sedes the old (II Corinthians 3:9ff., Hebrews 7:22, 8:13)—so much so that Luther could venture to speak of the "new deca-logues" which the perfect Christian, filled with the Spirit, could put in the place of Moses.[36] "If ye be led of the Spirit, ye are not under the law" (Galatians 5:18)—a word which in our ethics we have yet to discover, and which Methodism in particular, thanks to its legalist interpreters, has largely forgotten. But John Wesley knew it, and his practical Christianity points the way out of our perennial impasse between Nomism and Antino-mianism in the direction of the third article of the Creed. His brother Charles had learnt this in the hour of his conversion from Luther's comment on Galatians 2:20: "He that can utter this word *me* (sc. "who loved me and gave Himself for me") and apply it unto himself with a true and constant faith, as St. Paul did, shall be a good disputant with Paul against the law. And this manner of applying is the very true force and power of faith."[37] So to "apply" Christianity is the work of the Holy Spirit, and it takes the form of covenant—the new covenant, to be sure, which for Wesley has a key of its own, characteristically differ-ent, for instance, from that of the Calvinist tradition, and which is the embodiment of what Dean Craig called "the reality of the redeemed life."

The old "Directions to Penitents and Believers for Covenant-ing with God" are still not out of date: first, the notion of eter-nity before us; "second: make your choice; third: embark with Christ; fourth, resign and deliver up yourselves to God in Christ; fifth, confirm and complete all this by solemn covenants."[38] It has to be remembered, of course, that this is "returning" into, and "renewing" what God, on His part, has promised and kept from the beginning; it is but the human response to His ever-lasting covenant with His people. Our prayer for "revival" is: "O Lord, *revive Thy work* in the midst of the years, in the midst of the years make known" (Habakkuk 3:2). The dry bones of Ezek-iel's vision can only live if the Spirit of the Lord enters into

---

36. *Weimar Edition,* XXXIX.1.47; Theses *De Fide,* Nos. 51–6.

37. *Weimar Edition,* XL.I.297

38. Printed in *Order of Administration of the Sacraments . . . and Directions for Covenanting with God,* Wesleyan Conference Office (London, 1875).

them; or, to change the metaphor, a man rescued from drowning can only recover if there is still life in him—otherwise all respiratory exercises will be in vain. "All the arts of the revivalist" in Ronald Knox's travesty of Methodism never did and never will bring about revival; it is only on the basis of that which God has wrought that Wesley's secondary "exercises"—doing no harm, doing all good, attending upon the ordinances of God—have meaning and promise. Practical Christianity practises the "work of God" as *genetivus subjectivus;* to do His will is, as Wesley so often phrases it, to receive the stamp and seal of His Spirit; "for we are His workmanship, created in Christ Jesus *unto good* works, which God hath before ordained that we should walk in them" (Ephesians 2:10).

> Here then to Thee Thy own I leave;
> Mould as Thou wilt Thy passive clay;
> But let me all Thy stamp receive,
> But let me all Thy words obey,
> Serve with a single heart and eye,
> And to Thy glory live and die.[39]

39. *M.H.B.,* No. 572; cf. Isaiah 64:8, Jeremiah 18:4.

3

Missionary

Missionary Christianity is the synthesis of scriptural and practical Christianity; it is, in short, the practice of the Word, or, as Wesley says: "Scriptural Christianity, as beginning to exist in individuals; as spreading from one to another; as covering the earth."[1] The relevant portion of scripture here is, of course, the *Acts of the Apostles*, to which Wesley's *Journal* presents the commentary. "My word shall not return unto me void, but it shall accomplish that which I please, and it shall prosper in the thing whereto I sent it" (Isaiah 55:11); that "thing," for Wesley, is the change wrought in human lives, the "real," not only the "relative" change.[2] It is a thing with which the traditional practice of the Church has ceased to reckon, for it has ceased to expect anything to "happen" as a result of the foolishness of preaching. Consequently, the story of the *Acts* is written off as exceptional and slightly abnormal; while for Wesley it is literally and abidingly true that "the word of God increased, and the number of the disciples multiplied greatly" (Acts 6:7).

> When He first the work begun,
> Small and feeble was His day:
> Now the word doth swiftly run,
> Now it wins its widening way;
>
> • • •
>
> Sons of God, your Saviour praise!
> He the door hath opened wide;

1. *Works*, V.38.
2. Ibid., VI.45.

He hath given the word of grace,
Jesu's word is glorified![3]

Open, then, with me the *Journal* at random for a brief glance at the record of events in 1753. There is, as in the *Acts,* trouble and hostility in store for the Methodist preacher; the mob, quite often instigated by the clergy of the town, is ready to salute him in its own way. "I did not expect the mob at Nantwich . . . would be so quiet as that at Chester. We were saluted with curses and hard names, as soon as we entered the town."[4] Membership in the society, even association with the crowd that listens to Wesley, can cost a man his position: "I preached at Boothbank, where I met Mr. C., late gardener to the Earl of W. Surely it cannot be! Is it possible the Earl should turn off an honest, diligent, well-tried servant, who had been in the family above fifty years, for no other fault than hearing the Methodists?"[5] But the preacher is not deflected from his course. In Edinburgh "was now an open and effectual door, and not many adversaries. I could hear of none but a poor Seceder; who went up and down, and took much pains. But he did not see much fruit of his labor; the people would come and hear for themselves, both in the morning and in the afternoon."[6] The Gamaliel story comes to mind (Acts 5:38f.). And, again, the new tongues of Pentecost, when Mr. Walsh "preached in Irish in Moorfields. The congregation was exceeding large, and behaved seriously; though probably many of them came purely to hear what manner of language it was. For the sake of these he preached afterwards in English, if by any means he might gain some."[7] But such preaching is always "followed up" in the pastoral supervision of the hearers and the strict discipline of apostolic days (Acts 5:1–11, 8:18–24, I Corinthians 5): at St. Ives in Cornwall "I began examining the society; but I was soon obliged to stop short. I found an accursed thing among them: wellnigh one and all bought or sold uncustomed goods. I therefore delayed speaking

3. *M.H.B.,* No. 263.
4. *Journal,* 28th March 1753.
5. Ibid., 31st March 1753.
6. Ibid., 21st April 1753.
7. Ibid., 1st July 1753.

to any more till I had met them all together. This I did in the evening, and told them plain, either they must put this abomination away, or they would see my face no more. They severally promised so to do. So I trust this plague is stayed."[8]

The meaning of Evangelism is well expressed in Charles Wesley's "Epistle to the Revd Mr John Wesley" where, once again, his genius for theological definition comprises in a few lines (the last four quoted below) the whole purpose of the brothers' Mission:

> What then remains for us on earth to do,
> But labour on with Jesus in our view,
> Who bids us kindly for His patients care,
> Calls us the burden of His church to bear,
> To feed His flock, and nothing seek beside,
> And nothing know, but Jesus crucified?
>
> When first sent forth to minister the word,
> Say, did we preach ourselves, or Christ the Lord?
> Was it our aim disciples to collect,
> To raise a party, or to found a sect?
> No; but to spread the power of Jesu's name,
> Repair the walls of our Jerusalem
> Revive the piety of ancient days,
> And fill the earth with our Redeemer's praise.[9]

Thus the evangelist is, in the ancient phrase, the Gospeller, the man whose sole function is to record the facts of our salvation, to tell, as it were, "without note and comment," the tidings of that which God has done for us in Christ. Evangelism, so understood, can never be the field of specialists or the target of extraordinary years and seasons in Methodism; it is the "normal" work of the whole Church all the time—unless she has ceased, in truth and in deed, to be the Church of Christ.

The evangelist is sure of his apostolate. Wesley measures apostolic succession—in the phrase coined, I believe, by Mervyn Stockwood—by apostolic success. To "carry on His victory" is the motto of John's itinerant labors, as it is the key-note of so

8. Ibid., 25th and 27th July 1753.
9. *Poetical Works*, VI.63.

many of Charles's hymns; and it is not irreverent to picture the preacher on his horse, in the retinue and service of his triumphant Master, echoing in his own life the words of the 45th Psalm:

> Come, and maintain Thy righteous cause,
> And let Thy glorious toil succeed;
> Dispread the victory of Thy Cross,
> Ride on, and prosper in Thy deed;
> Through earth triumphantly ride on,
>   every heart alone.[10]

The means of this evangelism are twofold: extraordinary, devised by the Wesleys in their peculiar hour of grace; and ordinary, binding for all times. No rigid division, however, is implied here; the formation of societies, for instance, would cover both categories. Wesley "admired the original discipline of the primitive Church . . . he felt that his opportunity had come; he determined that he would use all his influence in attempting to realize in his societies the deep spiritual experiences of the members of the apostolic church."[11] Even in the national emergency of 1745, in the midst of war and rumors of war, he had to ignore the well-meant advice "to return to the Church, to renounce all his lay assistants, to dissolve his societies, to leave off field-preaching, and to accept honourable preferment."[12] Why? "1. Because the preacher cannot give proper exhortations and instructions to those who are convinced of sin, unless he has opportunities of meeting them apart from the mixed unawakened multitude. 2. They cannot watch over one another in love, unless they are thus united together. Nor, 3, can the believer build up one another and bear one another's burdens."[13] "I cannot understand how any minister can hope ever to give up his account with joy, unless, as Ignatius advises, he knows all his flock by name, not overlooking the menservants and the maidservants."[14]

10. *M.H.B.*, No. 270; see ibid., Nos. 246 and so on.
11. John S. Simon, *John Wesley and the Methodist Societies*, p. 49.
12. *Journal*, 23rd May 1745.
13. John S. Simon, *John Wesley and the Advance of Methodism*, p. 78.
14. *Journal*, 24th January 1743.

"Lay assistants" are next in importance. Telford, in his *History of Lay Preaching*,[15] has shown how both the warrant of scripture and the support of tradition are on Wesley's side, beginning with the sending of the Seventy in the Gospel (Luke 10:2) and their forerunners in the Old Testament. Yet, at least, the scale on which he recruited these forces in the service of Methodism was something of a revolution in Church history. Not only the weight of traditional prejudice, but even certain passages of scripture stood in his way; so, when he read "Let your women be silent in the churches, for it is not permitted them to speak," he had to comment: "unless they are under an extraordinary impulse of the Spirit."[16] Extraordinary circumstances, he held, demand extraordinary agents to spread the Gospel. It was, of course, not the secular idea of emancipation that he introduced into the household of the Church, but the Reformation doctrine of the common priesthood of believers, which he found in the New Testament and applied with unprecedented clarity and vigor to the needs of his day.

Neither was this done without safeguards. In his brother Charles, John had an ever-vigilant counsellor by his side, and the lay preachers a censor whom they had every reason to fear. Charles Wesley would insist "that no one be allowed to preach with us, till my brother and I have heard him with our own ears, and talked fully with him, and if needs be, to keep him with us some days"; which in an individual case meant "that he does not print any more of his nonsense, and that he does not introduce the use of his doggerel hymns in any of our societies. I cannot in conscience agree to his putting nonsense into their mouths."[17] Are we so sure that such caution is superfluous today, that Church visitation and check on preaching, as practised by the Reformers and by our fathers in the faith, are no longer needed? Have we not all had Charles Wesley's experience: "I heard him with pain. It was not so bad as I feared, nor so good as to make me believe him called to the work. . . . It was beyond all description. I can't say he preached false doctrine, or

15. Telford, *History of Lay Preaching*.
16. Wesley, *Notes on the New Testament*, I Corinthians 14:34.
17. Frank Baker, *Charles Wesley as Revealed in His Letters* (The Wesley Historical Society Lectures, No. 14, London, 1948), pp. 84, 86.

true, or any doctrine at all, but pure unmixed nonsense. He set my blood a-galloping, and threw me into such a sweat that I expected the fever to follow. Of this I am infallibly sure, that if ever he had a gift for preaching, he has now totally lost it."[18] And when John Wesley was prepared to argue that "grace" was perhaps more important than "gifts," Charles would retort: "Are not both indispensably necessary? Has not the cause suffered, in Ireland especially, through the insufficiency of the preachers? Should we not first regulate, reform, and bring into discipline the preachers we have, before we look for more?"[19]

Not more, but better preachers was then, as it is now, the paramount requirement of Methodism. There is no doubt whatever that sermons other than biblical would never have passed the Wesleys' test; nor that they would never have subscribed to the glib modern phrase that "the pastorate is vested in the laity." With that, we try to justify the uncritical perpetuation of the itinerant system—completely oblivious of the fact that Wesley's "Plan" presupposed a training and quality of lay leadership which to our generation has become almost legendary. What was the great and ingenious expedient of his time, allowing the ministers to live as travelling missionaries while the "locals" could safely be entrusted with the regular "watering" of the garden (I Corinthians 3:6), must in the absence of such forces result in a fatal weakening of our ministry; it must, by comparison with other denominations, be counted as one of the major "causes of the inefficacy of Christianity" in our midst. Modern conditions will, in fact, as American Methodism has been quick to recognize, force drastic corrections upon our traditional polity; churches in new housing areas, for instance, will not ever be really served or "built up" by any other device but that of the residential and permanent pastorate. John Wesley would be the first to see and say this; for his much-invoked genius of organization lay precisely in the flexibility of his missionary methods. And Charles Wesley represents in his own person the other form of the ministry (which early Methodism, counting so many "incumbents" among its members, always intended to preserve)

18. Ibid., pp. 82, 85.
19. Ibid., p. 83.

when he "sits down" to work in Bristol and London only, in a life-long intensified "cure of souls."[20]

I do not wish to be misunderstood. Far be it from me to question or belittle the historic role of Wesley's itinerancy, or to deny either its apostolic precedent or its contemporary usefulness. But usefulness, and not habit, must be the criterion in any Methodist appraisal and reappraisal of our system; and extraordinary agencies such as this cannot either be understood or continued without the extraordinary sense of urgency which compelled Wesley to mobilize his lay preachers, and which, in like measure, he demanded from each of them before admitting them to his pulpits. "What is the end of all ecclesiastical order? Is it not to bring souls from the power of Satan to God; and to build them up in His fear and love? Order, then, is so far valuable, as it answers these ends; and if it answers them not, it is nothing worth."[21] From this Wesley's lieutenants concluded: "Our Old Plan has been to follow the openings of Providence, and to alter and amend the plan, as we saw needful, in order to be more useful in the hand of God."[22]

We turn to the ordinary means of evangelism: the exposition of the Word and the administration of the Sacraments. It is a pagan England that Wesley has to face, as we have to face paganism today, open or concealed, in the so-called Christian countries on either side of the Atlantic. "Ask a countryman, What is faith? What is repentance? What is holiness? What is true religion?—and he is no more able to give you an intelligible answer, than if you were to ask him about the Northeast passage. If religion is not even in their heads, can it be in their hearts?"[23] It is even a pagan Oxford to which he has to speak from the University pulpit of St. Mary's: "Let us stand a little, and survey this strange sight, a Christian World. . . . First, I would ask, Where does this Christianity now exist? Where, I

20. Baker, *Charles Wesley as Revealed in His Letters,* pp. 117ff.

21. *Works,* XII.79. Note the form of the question discussed at the 1745 Conference: "Is episcopal, presbyterian or independent church government most agreeable to reason?"

22. Letter from Pawson to Atmore, 17th May 1791 (Newcastle vs. Hull District about the provision of the Sacrament); see George Smith, *History of Methodism* (1858), II.15.

23. *Works,* IX.225.

pray, do the Christians live? Which is the country, the inhabitants whereof are all thus filled with the Holy Ghost? . . . Let me ask you then, in tender love, and in the spirit of meekness, Is this a Christian city? Is Christianity, Scriptural Christianity, found here? . . . Are all the Magistrates, all Heads and Governors of Colleges and Halls, and their respective Societies (not to speak of the inhabitants of the town), of one heart and one soul?"[24] No wonder that "the Beadle came to me afterwards, and told me the Vice-Chancellor had sent him for my notes. I sent them without delay, not without admiring the wise providence of God. Perhaps few men of note would have given a sermon of mine the reading, if I had put it in their hands; but by this means it came to be read, probably more than once, by every man of eminence in the University."[25]

Evidently Wesley was understood without an interpreter. We, who in our generation have become almost obsessed with "the problem of communication" and curiously involved even in our descriptions of it, may well pause to reflect that for him, the most successful evangelist of modern Church history, this problem as such just does not seem to have existed. For when analysis has finished its work, when all is said and done that can be said and done by way of explanation, mediation, and adjustment, there comes a point where further translation is impossible; and Wesley always comes to that point at once: it is the name of Jesus Christ Himself who is the same yesterday, and today, and for ever. In every age it is this Jesus and none other (II Corinthians 11:4, Acts 4:12) with whom the hearer of the Gospel is presented; and to be sure of the content of this presentation is far more important than to be absorbed in its technique. "He who submits himself," says Bengel, "to the constraining influence of Divine Love in the search after Divine Truth, imbibes from the Divine Words, when he once perceived their meaning, all things profitable for salvation, without labor, and without stimulus";[26] therefore he felt that he could dispense with any moral or casuistic "application" in his *Notes on the*

24. *Works*, V.45, 47, 48.
25. *Journal*, 24th August 1744.
26. Bengel, *Gnomon*, I.65.

New Testament. The Word of God is sufficient to speak for itself and to see to its own success.

Of course John Wesley had his own method. "What is the best general method of preaching? To invite; to convince; to offer Christ; to build up; and to do this in some measure in every sermon."[27] And his brother provided him with an additional means of communication which ever since has proved its singular efficiency: the Methodists sing their faith. Whatever the critics may say, the fact remains that Charles Wesley enabled "plain, unlettered men" to be at home in the solid theology of his hymns, and so to lay hold upon the fullness of the Gospel. "Our poet, true to the mission of Methodism, makes experience the connecting link between knowledge and practice, and devotes an entire section of his work to 'Hymns and Prayers to the Trinity,' in which the doctrine is presented in most intimate connection with his own spiritual interests, and those of his readers. Such a mode of treating it is the best answer to those who represent it as a mere metaphysical speculation devoid of practical interest. . . . The 'higher Christian life' is thus shown to be dependent upon the highest revealed mysteries, and these in their turn minister illumination, help, and comfort to the humblest believer who receives the testimony of God concerning His Son."[28] The hymnody of the nineteenth and twentieth centuries has nothing to offer in comparison with that; and we may as well admit that the depth of Charles Wesley's experience is altogether beyond most of us. But this is no reason to suspend the use of his hymns today. Peter Böhler's advice, slightly paraphrased, is still applicable: "Sing the faith until thou hast it, and then sing it because thou hast it!"

What is the apostolic preaching that was so spread and sung throughout the British Isles and America? Nothing other than the Christ of the scriptures, Christ incarnate, Christ crucified, risen and ascended. Once again the whole kerygma of the Acts could be traced throughout the Wesley hymns; but there is only time for the briefest hint at the Easter section. Here is the biblical unity of the Cross and the resurrection; the Lamb that was slain and the Lion that prevailed; the fulfilment of the Exodus

27. *Works*, VIII.317
28. Editor's Preface in *Poetical Works*, VII.204.

and Red Sea story in the passover of the New Testament and the victory of the third day; the triumphant shout of the Great Deliverer (Wesley's favorite epithet for Jesus) and the inauguration of His Kingdom in the messianic promises of Psalms 2 and 45; here is the unfolding of His ministry as prophet, priest, and king, the Pauline notion that we are more than conquerors through Him that loved us, and the anticipation of Aulen's concept of the *Christus Victor* who has spoiled principalities and powers.[29] This is full of practical consequences: Sunday is restored to its original meaning as the day of the resurrection and of the "applied" power of the living Christ;[30] and the working day, even of the aging and failing John Wesley, is seen in the same light: "If you and I should be called hence this year, we may bless God that we have not lived in vain. Come let us have a few more strokes at Satan's kingdom, and then we shall depart in peace!"[31] And in praying to "Jesus, our hope," turning to Him as our great High Priest and Intercessor, Charles Wesley recognizes the centrality of the Epistle to the Hebrews and recovers for us the proper place of the Ascension in the year of the Church and the life of the believer:

> Entered the holy place above,
> Covered with meritorious scars,
> The tokens of His dying love
> Our great High-priest in glory bears;
> He pleads His passion on the tree,
> He shows Himself to God for me.

> Before the throne my Saviour stands,
> My Friend and Advocate appears;
> My name is graven on His hands,
> And Him the Father always hears;
> While low at Jesu's Cross I bow,
> He hears the blood of sprinkling now.
> This instant now I may receive
> The answer of His Powerful prayer;

29. The hymns here alluded to are *M.H.B.*, Nos. 481, 411, 412, 243, 270, 97, 246, and so on.
30. *M.H.B.*, No. 661.
31. *Letters*, VIII.197.

This instant now by Him I live,
His prevalence with God declare;
And soon my spirit, in His hands,
Shall stand where my Forerunner stands.[32]

This hymn is taken from the "Select Passages of Holy Scripture"; it should be sung, of course, at the Eucharist. For here is the real presence of Him who ever liveth to make intercession for us, and the closest link between the worship of the Church ("while low at Jesu's Cross I bow") and His eternal sacrifice ("He hears the blood of sprinkling now"). In the notion of this sacrifice, as represented and re-claimed by our own, Charles Wesley, following Brevint, goes considerably farther than the Reformers; whether he also goes beyond that which is written in Hebrews and at the beginning of Romans 12 has yet to be carefully explored, and if he does, he will stand corrected by the scriptures. Here he is manifestly indebted to the teaching of the Anglican Mother Church; but more than one influence is at work in the development of his eucharistic doctrine. On the surface (see the Thirty-nine [25] Articles)—there are traces of the Calvinist position; but far more significant—at least to an ex-Lutheran!—is the kinship with Luther in the direct identification of Christ's Body and Blood with the elements, in the literal obedience to the command and promise of the words of institution, in the insistence upon the mystery that calls for adoration, not inquiry, and in the notion of the Sacrament as the "chiefest" means of grace by which the omnipresent God makes His binding appointment with us. It is clearly impossible to classify the Wesleys with the label of any party or school; learning from many traditions, they have still more to teach them all, and Protestants have particular need to be reminded that the sacrament was never meant to become a quarterly funereal occasion, but—

With high and heavenly bliss
Thou dost our spirits cheer;
Thy house of banqueting is this,
And Thou hast brought us here.[33]

32. *M.H.B.*, No. 232; cf. also No. 561.
33. *M.H.B.*, No. 761.

This, again, is scriptural Christianity; it is the Master Himself in the Gospel who likens His Kingdom to a marriage feast; it is the primitive Church from which Wesley takes the usage of invoking *(epiklesis)* the Holy Spirit's power over the elements;[34]

> Come, Holy Ghost, Thine influence shed,
> And realize the sign;
> Thy life infuse into the bread,
> Thy power into the wine.

and it is the general practice of the Acts to "continue daily . . . breaking bread" (2:46). Hence the "Duty of Constant Communion," firmly established in Wesley's own life,[35] is incumbent upon the Methodist people. Their hunger for the Word of God was, from the beginning, a hunger for the bread of life in its *audible and visible* form; and where would American Methodism be without the clamour of Asbury's people for the administration of the sacrament by the hands of their own preachers? No less than 166 Hymns on the Lord's Supper were written by Charles Wesley to meet the need of the large communicant congregations; and the day will come when we shall extract them from the dusty volumes of the *Poetical Works* and make them, in hymn-sheets or supplements, available for the whole Church. If Wesley is right in regarding the sacrament as a converting, not merely confirming ordinance, then it has to be treated seriously among the means of evangelism, and in the eucharistic hymns he has left us invaluable tools for the discharge of our missionary task.

For the motive of this evangelism we have not far to look. One hymn, translated by John Wesley from the German,[36] contains all the essential guiding factors of his mission, and a glance at each of the five verses reveals, incidentally, something like a neat compendium of Pauline theology:

> Shall I for fear of feeble man,
> The Spirit's course in me restrain?

34. *M.H.B.*, No. 765, and particularly No. 767:

35. "We may state with reasonable confidence that, throughout his apostolic life, Wesley approached the Table of the Lord once in about very five days." T. H. Barratt, *Methodism: Its Present Responsibilities*, p. 73.

36. *M.H.B.*, No. 783 (by Johann Joseph Winckler).

> Or, undismayed, in deed and word
> Be a true witness for my Lord?

"Though we, or an angel from heaven, preach any other Gospel unto you . . . let him be accursed," wrote Paul to the Galatians (1:8), and what the Nomists did to his work there, the Antinomians did to Wesley's. But he goes on, with the Apostle: "If I yet pleased men, I should not be the servant of Christ" (1:10); and his warning remains pertinent that any preacher who becomes—or any Church system which makes him—a "Yes-Man" to the people, is guilty of betraying the cause of Christ.

> Saviour of men, Thy searching eye
> Doth all my inmost thoughts descry;
> Doth aught on earth my wishes raise,
> Or the world's pleasures or its praise?

The face that is so bold toward the world changes completely in the sight of God, where he "would not lift up so much as his eyes unto heaven" (Luke 18:13). When he stands before Him unto whom all hearts be open, all desires known, and from whom no secrets are hid, Wesley says with the Apostle: "I know nothing by myself; yet am I not hereby justified; but he that judgeth me is the Lord" (I Corinthians 4:4). The witness of Christ, unafraid of the world's verdict, is not saved by the sense of his own innocence, but by grace alone.

> The love of Christ doth me constrain
> To seek the wandering souls of men;
> With cries, entreaties, tears, to save,
> To snatch therefrom the gaping grave.

As he himself was the "brand, plucked from eternal fire," so his life-long "business," and that of his helpers, is to save souls;[37] and in this passionate concern—to use the phrase from an old German Lutheran ordinal—"no soul must be given up." Whether Wesley proclaims the constraining love of Christ (II Corinthians 5:14) or urges sinners to flee from the wrath to

37. *Works*, VIII.310, 11.

come (I Thessalonians 1:10; Luke 13:3; Acts 2:40), is merely a difference of key; it is the same instrument which he plays with all the powers at his command, to the glory of God and the salvation of his fellow men.

> My life, my blood, I here present,
> If for Thy truth they may be spent;
> Fulfil Thy sovereign counsel, Lord;
> Thy will be done, Thy name adored.

"And here we offer and present unto Thee, O Lord, ourselves, our souls and bodies, to be a reasonable, holy, and living sacrifice unto Thee" (cf. Romans 12:1). We note the sacramental meaning of the passage and the personal implications, for Wesley, of "being spent" in the Master's service. Preaching the word or administering the sacrament, the minister is never more nor less than the hand through which the gift is distributed—an activity best described as "dispensing" the means of grace or "rightly dividing the word of truth" (II Timothy 2:15).

> Give me Thy strength, O God of power;
> Then, let winds blow or thunders roar,
> Thy faithful witness will I be:
> 'Tis fixed; I can do all through Thee!

"In the children of God, repentance and faith exactly answer each other. . . . Repentance says, 'Without Him I can do nothing'; Faith says, 'I can do all things through Christ strengthening me'";[38] and the unity of these two affirmations is the key to Wesley's missionary "drive." So, with the concluding note from Philippians 4:13, the previous quotations are fittingly summed up. Taken from Galatians in the first verse; I and II Corinthians in the third; I Thessalonians and Timothy in the fourth, they form indeed a complete, though unintentional, reproduction of St. Paul.

Pauline, too, is the universal range of this evangelism. It would not be truly apostolic, if it did not reach Jew and Gentile, Churchman and outsider alike. In the very hour of conversion,

38. *Works*, V.168. Cf. *M.H.B.*, No. 785.

when the lips of Charles Wesley are touched ("redeemed," in Luther's translation of Psalm 71:23) and his "wondering soul" begins to sing like a bird released from its cage (cf. Psalm 51:15), he must share the newly found righteousness and deliverance (Psalms 40:10; 31:1) with the "outcasts of men" the "harlots, publicans, and thieves."[39] For God "will have all men to be saved, and to come unto the knowledge of the truth" (I Timothy 2:4). This, and this only, is Wesley's "Arminianism," the corrective, as George Croft Cell has taught us, of the Calvinist extreme; it is not the introduction of crypto-Pelagian elements into the concept of the saving faith. In 1749 Wesley and Whitefield reached agreement, while retaining their several positions, "not to preach controversially either for or against absolute election, irresistible grace, or final perseverance . . . [and] continually to maintain that man's whole salvation is of God, and his whole damnation of himself."[40]

"If our Gospel be hid, it is hid to them that are lost" (II Corinthians 4:3). The preacher has no control over the response; his sole commission is to deliver the message. But Wesley had every reason to rejoice over "how great a flame" had been "kindled by a spark of grace," how "the door" had "opened wide"; and from the results he saw in his own lifetime, he could make bold to predict:

> Saw ye not the cloud arise,
> Little as a human hand?
> Now it spreads along the skies,
> Hangs o'er all the thirsty land:
> Lo! the promise of a shower
> Drops already from above;
> But the Lord will shortly pour
> All the Spirit of His love![41]

It is not written that all will accept the Gospel, but that all shall hear it before the end comes (Matthew 24:14, Romans 9:16ff.); and in the threefold parable of flame, door, and cloud,

39. *M.H.B.*, No. 361. The point in Luther's translation is *"meine Lippen, die du erlöset hast";* and "deliver me *in* Thy righteousness" is his fundamental discovery.
40. John S. Simon, *John Wesley and the Advance of Methodism*, p. 166.
41. *M.H.B.*, No. 263.

Wesley sketches, as it were, the outline of a truly biblical doctrine of progress in Church history. We speak, with Wesley, of "results"; but we ought, at once, to revert to the singular and remember that there is only one genuine aim and outcome of all evangelism—namely, "that we may present every man perfect in Christ Jesus" (Colossians 1:28). The man of God, as we saw earlier, is the product of the word of God (II Timothy 3:17, James 1:18); and Wesley has a vital interest in the "finished" product, the transformation which must follow upon conversion (II Corinthians 3:18), in short, in Christian perfection. The quest for holiness remains the great theme of his life, redirected, but not interrupted, by the Aldersgate event,[42] and it springs directly from his reading of the New Testament. His immediate reaction to the great commandments of our Lord, sharpened by the study of William Law, is, significantly, not, as ours would be, "then it is impossible to be a Christian," but, "then it is impossible to be a half-Christian!"[43] Several key texts hold him in their grip—the holiness without which no man shall see the Lord (Hebrews 12:14), the God of peace who will sanctify you wholly and preserve blameless (I Thessalonians 5:23), the mind that was in Christ (Philippians 2:5), the perfect disciple that shall be as his Master (Luke 6:40), the man born of God who cannot commit sin (I John 3:9), the perfect love which casteth out fear (I John 4:18).

No Methodist preaching without the preaching of perfect love;[44] but (the Conference of 1758) "In what manner would you advise those, who think they have attained, to speak of their experience? A. With great wariness, and with the deepest humility and self-abasement before God. Q. How should young preachers especially speak of perfection in public? A. Not too minutely or circumstantially, but rather in general and scriptural terms.—It follows that the most perfect have continual need of the merits of Christ, even for their actual transgressions, and may well say

42. "In 1737 they saw holiness comes by faith. They saw likewise, that men are justified before they are sanctified; but still holiness was their point." *Works*, VIII.300.

43. Ibid., XI.367.

44. "If we can prove that any of our Local Preachers or Leaders, either directly or indirectly, speak against it, let him be a Local Preacher or Leader no longer. I doubt whether he shall continue in the Society." *Letters*, VIII.249.

for themselves, as well as their brethren, 'Forgive us our tres-
passes.'"[45] If there is a "second work of grace," its only scriptural
warrant is that which Charles Wesley found in Matthew 8:4:

> Whene'er Thou dost Thy grace bestow,
> Lest proudly I the blessing show,
> A second grace impart,
> "Tell it to none"—with vain delight,
> "Tell it to none,"—in mercy write
> Upon my broken heart.[46]

"You make sinless perfection necessary after justification, in
order to make us meet for glory," is one of the current charges
against John Wesley; and his rejoinder: "And who does not? Indeed, men do not agree in the time. Some believe it is attained
before death; some in the article of death; some in an after-state,
in the Mystic or the Popish purgatory. But all writers whom I
have ever seen till now (the Romish themselves not excepted)
agree that we must be 'fully cleansed from all sin' before we can
enter into glory."[47] At least in the matter of timing the attainment, he leaves room, we note, for tolerance of differing "opinions";[48] and when pressed, at the end of his life, for his own personal account of the sanctified state, John Wesley, after some
hesitation, answers by quoting his brother's prayer:

> Jesus, confirm my heart's desire
> To work, and speak, and think for Thee;
> Still let me guard the holy fire,
> And still stir up Thy gift in me.
>
> Ready for all Thy perfect will,
> My acts of faith and love repeat,
> Till death Thy endless mercies seal,
> And make the sacrifice complete.[49]

45. John S. Simon, *John Wesley, the Master Builder,* p. 50.
46. *Poetical Works,* X.210.
47. *Letters,* II.226.
48. "Always drawing, rather than driving" is another relevant piece of advice about the manner of preaching sanctification (*Works,* XI.387).
49. *M.H.B.,* No. 386. The story is found in Mouzon, *Fundamentals of Methodism* (1923), p. 68.

To those who "cannot reconcile some parts of my behaviour with the character I have long supported," he replies: "I have disclaimed that character on every possible occasion. I told all in our ship, all at Savannah, all at Frederica, and that over and over, in express terms, 'I am not a Christian. I only follow after, if haply I attain it.'"[50] Of the plerophory of faith, he admits even after his conversion: "This witness of the Spirit I have not, but I patiently wait for it. . . . Those who have not yet received joy in the Holy Ghost, the love of God, and the *plerophory* of faith, I believe to be Christians in that imperfect sense wherein I may call myself such."[51]

These testimonies, which could easily be augmented,[52] should act as what Wesley called in another connection "a preservative against unsettled notions in religion." It must not be forgotten that Philippians 3:12, "not as though I had already attained," is the text for the "Standard Sermon on Christian Perfection." And precisely in the place where he began, the task of rethinking this "grand depositum" of Methodism[53] must be taken up. There is, above all, a most urgent need for biblical reorientation. Perfection, like the God of Pascal, has to be freed from the absolutism of the philosophers and interpreted in the light of Abraham, Isaac, and Jacob, of the "perfect man" in the Old Testament (Kings, Psalms, Proverbs), and the perfect disciple in the New. It is not the blueprint of one standardized "type" for all, but the renewal of the individual after the image of Jesus Christ; again, no subtle salvationist egotism, but the "social religion" of Wesley extended to the area of sanctification.[54] "The opinion I have concerning it (sc. perfection) at present, I espouse because I think it scriptural. If therefore I am convinced it is not scriptural, I shall willingly relinquish it . . . avoid setting perfection too high or too low; setting it just as high as the Scripture does."[55] Lest it be set

50. *Letters*, I.284f.
51. Ibid., I.264.
52. They are not really outweighed by the evidence on the other side with which Roy S. Nicholson (*The Asbury Seminarian*, 1952, VI, No. 1, pp. 64–89) has tried to defend his case for "John Wesley's personal experience of Christian perfection."
53. *Letters*, VIII.238.
54. *Works*, V.296–8.
55. *Works*, XI.450, 397.

too high, John Wesley speaks of God's "imitable perfections";[56] lest it be set too low, Charles Wesley vows:

> Wherefore to Him my feet shall run,
> My eyes on His perfections gaze,
> My soul shall live for God alone,
> And all within me shout His praise.[57]

In this turn from my to His perfection lies the most important single correction which Charles Wesley administers to his brother's statements. Where John incessantly questions himself and others about the degree of salvation up to date, Charles is silent; where John readily accepts self-evidence from those who claim attainment, Charles remains sceptical;

> Can confident assertions prove
> The truth of your abundant grace?
> Ye talkers of your perfect love,
> Your pure consummate holiness;
> So highly who yourselves esteem,
> And make yourselves your endless theme.[58]

where John insists upon his time-table which fixes the reaching of the goal at "five minutes before death" at the latest, Charles maintains:

> Nor charge Thee with delay;
> Do with me, Lord, as seems Thee meet,
> But let me always Pray.[59]

Prayer thus takes the place of pressure and makes an end to reflection. Otherwise the doctrine must become unbearable in experience and scripturally unsound. As there is no warrant for the "Mystic or Popish purgatory," so there is none for John Wesley's own timing of the terminal, nor indeed for the opposite

56. *Works*, VIII.352.
57. *M.H.B.*, No. 384.
58. *Poetical Works*, IX.353 (on Proverbs 27:2: "Let another man praise thee"); cf. ibid., p. 57 (on Exodus 34:34).
59. Ibid., II.103.

error of our modern relativists who deny any chance of Christian Perfection this side of eternity. All these attempts to fix the hour, early or late, in this world or the next, are but different forms of the same dogmatism which leads us from the act of prayer and faith into the realm of conjecture and reflection. Charles Wesley had not so learned Christ; he found in the New Testament that the strongest "perfectionist" expressions occur in the concluding prayers with which the writers of the epistles commend their churches "unto Him that is able to keep you from falling, and to present you faultless before the presence of His glory with exceeding joy" (Jude 24; cf. Hebrews 13:20–1, I Thessalonians 5:23, Ephesians 3:20–1). So, in the words "I know thy works" (Revelations 2:2), he discovers the truth which makes us free:

> Less goodness in himself conceives
> Than Christ doth of His servant know;
> Who saved from self-reflection lives,
> Unconscious of the grace bestow'd,
> Simply resign'd, and lost in God.
>
> Himself he cannot perfect call,
> Or to the meanest saint prefer,
> Meanest himself, and least of all:
> And when the glorious character
> His spotless soul with Christ receives,
> His state to that great day he leaves.[60]

That is perfection by faith. It is, of course, what John Wesley himself believed: "I cannot doubt but that believers who wait and pray for it will find these scriptures fulfilled in themselves. My hope is that they will be fulfilled in me; I build on Christ, the Rock of Ages; on His sure mercies described in His Word; and on His promises, all which I know are Yea and Amen."[61] It is what Luther taught: "The Holy Ghost maketh me holy through the word and the sacraments which are in the Church and will

---

60. *Poetical Works*, XIII.222; cf. also X.395 (on Matthew 25:37): *I want that unreflecting love/Which simply Thy command obeys,/Content, if Thou at last approve,/Nor fondly on the action stays. . . .*

61. *Letters*, I.264.

make me perfectly holy on the last day."[62] Time and manner is for Him to determine "who has begun the good work in you and will perform it until the day of Jesus Christ" (Philippians 1:6); and only through the *Spiritus Sanctificator* can:

> Finish then Thy new creation,
> Pure and spotless let us be;
> Let us see Thy great salvation,
> Perfectly restored in Thee;
> Changed from glory into glory,
> Till in heaven we take our place,
> Till we cast our crowns before Thee,
> Lost in wonder, love, and praise.[63]

62. Luther, *Works (Weimar Edition)*, XXX.I.94.
63. *M.H.B.*, No. 431.

4

Catholic

"That we may present every man perfect in Christ" was the practical conclusion of the Wesleys' missionary Christianity. It is also the expression of their scriptural catholicity. "Every man," "perfect"—the emphasis lay both on the universality and the finished work of grace. Now we have to underline "in Christ." The mission of Methodism could and can have no other aim than to "present" men and women directly to Him, to win "real scriptural Christians"[1] rather than "good Methodists," to work across all party lines and sectarian labels—in Wesley's own phrase, "to assist all parties without forming any."[2] It is of the essence of this "movement" to be catholic as it is evangelical, and both, as we have seen, not by way of any special emphasis or organized campaign, but by the very nature of Methodism. "The Methodists are to spread life among all denominations; which they will do till they form a separate sect."[3]

But they did form a separate sect; and so the question must arise: how can this be justified? Has the movement, perhaps, run its course and exhausted its mission, so that, having gained its teleological end, the historic end of Methodism is now in sight? It would be tempting to write a paper or even a small book under the title, *If Charles Wesley Had His Way,* and to speculate upon the possible development of the "society" had it followed his guidance and remained within the Anglican body. "My chief concern upon earth, I said, was the prosperity of the

1. *Letters*, VIII.47.
2. Ibid., p. 71.
3. Ibid., p. 211.

Church of England; my next, that of the Methodists; my third, that of the preachers; that, if their interests should ever come in competition, I would give up the preachers for the good of the whole body of the Church of England; that nothing could ever force me to leave the Methodists but their leaving the Church."[4] We must be forever thankful that John Wesley's counsel prevailed, that he did ordain his preachers for America, and that the danger of becoming "a formal sect," which he and his brother predicted with such apprehension, did not, in fact, overtake the young independent Church—at least not until, in much more recent days, some Methodists renounced their catholic Christianity in favor of the narrow concept of "chapel" versus "church." Loss of fire had been the great defect of the eighteenth-century Church which Wesley was sent to repair; loss of form the weakness of the nineteenth-century "slide" into nonconformity; loss of substance seems to threaten Methodism now in the century of the ecumenical movement. This is, of course, an over-simplification of the issues; but it is clear that the sectarian danger today is not confined to one single direction, and that no easy short-cut is open to us by which we could reverse the course of history. The Church of England, as we know it, is not the same as that which the Wesleys called their mother; it is not, in any decisive sense, the Church of the Reformation, the Book of Common Prayer, the Homilies and the Articles; other forces have long since filled the vacuum of the Methodist exodus and determined the real life of Anglicanism. They have now vindicated John Wesley's action and prophecy: "I know the original doctrines of the Church are sound; I know her worship is (in the main) pure and scriptural. But if the essence of the Church of England, considered as such, consists in her orders and laws (many of which I myself can say nothing for) and not in her worship and doctrine, those who separate from her have a far stronger plea than I was ever sensible of."[5]

Therefore, we have to beware of a pseudo-catholic concept of unity which offers itself as the *via media* between Geneva and Rome but is, in fact, not so much "ecumenical" as peculiarly British and insular. To put orders and laws first is already, as

---

4. Frank Baker, *Charles Wesley as Revealed by His Letters*, pp. 102–3.
5. *Letters*, III.146.

Wesley knew well, to begin at the wrong end. "Although a difference in opinions or modes of worship may prevent an entire external union, yet need it prevent our union in affection? Though we cannot think alike, may we not love alike? May we not be of one heart, though we are not of one opinion? Without doubt we may. Herein all the children of God may unite."[6] The much-invoked "scandal of our divisions" does not lie at all where it is most often sought: "It is not division in respect of church government and procedures that is chiefly deplorable; this may even have a certain strategic value. What is deplorable is the divisive spirit which prevents the various divisions from working together, as they should, for the one purpose of making Christ supreme in the world. In a very real sense the true Church is 'one Church.' Organization, government, procedures, name—these are secondary.... Do two moribund churches become one dynamic church by the simple device of swallowing each other up?"[7]

In the present situation it is necessary, though not altogether edifying, to give our attention to this popular misconception of catholicity, of which Edwin Lewis thus warns us and which confronts Methodism, at least in Britain, with a decision of some gravity. The Archbishop of Canterbury, in a sermon of 1946, suggested that the non-episcopal Churches might consider "taking episcopacy into their system" as a first step toward the establishment of full communion with the Church of England. Discussions have proceeded on this basis, and reports have been published; no vote has so far been taken on either side, and the Free Churches await now (1954) the next move from the Anglican convocations.

• • •

[Since this was written, the Convocations of Canterbury and York have met (July 1955), and conversations between Anglicans and Methodists are about to begin in the near future. Materially nothing has changed. The Anglican position as recently stated by the Archbishop of Canterbury (in *The Server*, 10th July 1955) is: full communion with all Anglicans, full intercommunion with the Old Catholics, limited intercommunion with South

6. *Works*, V.493.
7. Edwin Lewis, *The Creator and the Adversary*, pp. 256–258.

India and Sweden. For the non-Anglican it is a little difficult to see what this offer has in common with the invitation of our Lord (John 6:35–7, Revelation 22:17) and how it can possibly help to end "the scandal of our divisions at the Lord's Table." It is still more difficult to see how Methodists, in their purely emotional response to the statement that they, too, are within the Body of Christ (!), have so completely failed to grasp the theological implications of the forthcoming talks. Are we quite sure—or content in the end to be told by our delegates—that Christ's way to unity is the making of Bishops, that the hands to make them must be Anglican, and that the finished article will be the true father-in-God? But the real issue is not: Bishops or Chairmen? It is: Lord's Supper or Church's Supper?[8] This is the hour of which Bernard Manning warned us:

> We cannot doubt that the Anglicans will offer sooner or later very favorable terms to the Methodists. They would meet the Methodists everywhere except on the fundamental issue. The Methodists would have to admit that full salvation comes by bishops alone— but anything else that they want they would get. . . . It is the ancient battle fought by St. Paul against them of the circumcision which our fathers fought and which we fight. Is God's grace legally conditioned? Is episcopacy in the new dispensation what circumcision was in the old? Is episcopacy the essential channel for the full blessing of the new Covenant in Christ as circumcision was the essential channel for the old Covenant in Moses? My friends in the Anglican Body do not like me to ask that question in those terms because, asked in those terms, it answers itself. But that—shall there be a new circumcision, a new legalism, under the Gospel?—is the issue between us and the Episcopalians, Anglican, Greek or Roman.[9]]

• • •

American Methodists must recognize a striking similarity between Dr. Fisher's proposal and that submitted by Thomas Coke early in the last century. He, too, thought, though acting only in his own name and by private correspondences, that for the sake of union he and Asbury should accept episcopal orders at the hands of Anglican Bishops, in addition to those con-

8. Edmund Schlik, *The Student World* (1950), pp. 46ff.
9. *Essays in Orthodox Dissent,* pp. 145, 142.

ferred by Wesley; and in his self-defense, after having failed with both sides, one can hear, above the tenor of apology and qualification, the descant so familiar to us from contemporary ecumenical argument: "I had provided in the fullest manner, in my indispensably necessary conditions, for the security, and, I may say, for the independence of our discipline and places of worship; but thought (perhaps erroneously, and I believe so now) that our field of action would have been exceedingly enlarged by that junction. If it be granted that my plan of union with the old Episcopal Church was desirable (which now, I think, was not so, though I most sincerely believed it to be so at that time), then if the plan could not have been accomplished without a repetition of the imposition of hands for the same office, I did believe, and do now believe, and have no doubt that *the repetition of the imposition of hands would have been perfectly justifiable for the enlargement of the field of action, etc., and would not, by any means, have invalidated the former consecration or imposition of hands.* Therefore I have no doubt but my consecration of Bishop Asbury was perfectly valid, and would have been so even if he had been reconsecrated. I never did apply to the general convention or any other convention for reconsecration. I never intended that either Bishop Asbury or myself should give up our episcopal office if the junction were to take place; but I should have had no scruple then, nor should I now, if the junction were desirable, to have submitted to, or to submit to, a reimposition of hands in order to accomplish a great object; but I do say again, I do not now believe such a junction desirable."[10]

You may well give thanks that Francis Asbury and not Thomas Coke steered the course of the Methodist Church in America; or does this seem a small matter? Will a future General Conference go back on the decisions against Coke in 1808 and fall for what an Anglican Bishop himself has called "episcopal inoculation," and what is, in fact, the new form of the circumcision denounced in Galatians 2 and Acts 15? Let me quote the unanimous resolution adopted by the Methodist Synod in Scotland in May 1953:

10. Letter to the General Conference of 1808, in Stevens, *History of the Methodist Church*, IV.443–4.

> That this Synod,
> Faithful to the catholic spirit of the Wesleys,
> Mindful that the altar is the Lord's Table,
> and therefore practicing intercommunion with all who
>   love Him in sincerity,
> feels bound to resent and resist the suggestion that the
>   right
> of full communion, which He Himself has granted to every
>   believer, should be made dependent upon a condition of
>   Church polity which is
> absent from the Gospel and alien to the principles of the
>   Reformation,
> unworthy of our Methodist heritage and disruptive of our
>   present unity,
> insular in its validity and irrelevant to the urgency of our
>   evangelistic mission.

No one is in a stronger position to endorse this motion than the Methodist Church in America. Who will make us believe that Seabury's consecration in 1784 was "valid," while Asbury's, in the same year, was not?—in other words, that the "apostolic succession" includes Henry the Eighth but not John Wesley? William Phoebus wrote in 1804: "Every scriptural qualification he (Wesley) certainly possessed, and if any term of human invention is attached to that order, he had every reasonable qualification. He could rule among his preachers with a word! He had literature. He had age, being one of the oldest Presbyters in England. He had souls to his apostleship—who has had so many, since the days of St. Peter and St. Paul?" Then follows an account of Methodist orders, no word of which we can afford to omit or to unsay today: "In the year of our Lord 1785, and in the ninth year of the Independence of the United States, on the first day of January, we thought it not robbery to call our Society a Church, having in it, and of it, several Presbyters and a President. Francis Asbury was ordained Deacon; having used the office some time, was ordained a Presbyter; having used that office well, was accounted worthy of double honor; and consecrated Prime Minister of the Methodist Episcopal Church in America. . . . The Methodists in America have as good a Presbyterian Ordination as any in the world (for a sufficient number of Presbyters have been always

74

present at the time of ordaining, from the day we first began, until now). And as good an Episcopal Ordination as any in the world, while one of Father Wesley's successors is with her (i.e. with the Church), vested with apostolic authority, being in a land where merit may rise. . . . I exhort my brethren to be courageous, and never to be ashamed to declare themselves the Ministers of Christ, through the medium of our apostle Wesley, and to keep an eye to that succession, and know, and let the people know, that God has given power to His Ministers, to declare and pronounce to His people, being penitent, the privileges of the Gospel."[11]

To "take into our system," *as a prerequisite for intercommunion,* any episcopacy other than the one which we have already received, would be a betrayal of the Gospel and a fatal misreading of our whole past, present and future. Of the past, because in the solemn hour of ordination we took "authority to fulfill the office of a minister *in the Church of Christ*"; therefore, as William Phoebus again points out, "who can reordain a man who had been ordained by our evangelist, or superintendent, without a breach of order, or who receive reordination and be innocent?"[12] Of the present, because episcopacy, actually taken into the system of such Churches as that of South India, or present already in the ancient success of the Swedish Lutherans, has made no practical difference whatever in regard to full communion with Canterbury. Of the future, because the acceptance of Dr. Fisher's proposal would ultimately reduce Methodism once more to the status of a "society," with a predominantly pietistic "emphasis." We should gain external union and lose the substance of our churchmanship. We should quote Charles Wesley, only to move yet farther away from his real legacy. We should "return"; yet not into the true unity of Christ's Church, but into those "entanglements" from which, as Wesley wrote "to our brethren in America," "God has so strangely made them free."[13]

11. See William Myles, *A Chronological History of the People called Methodists* (London 1813), pp. 164–165.

12. *An Essay on the Doctrine and Order of the Evangelical Church of America* (New York, 1817), p. 107.

13. *Letters*, VII.239.

What, then, is the right step for us to take? "I do not mean, 'Embrace my modes of worship;' or, 'I will embrace you.' This also is a thing which does not depend either on your choice or mine. We must both act as each is fully persuaded in his own mind. Hold you fast that which you believe is most acceptable to God, and I will do the same. . . . I have no desire to dispute with you one moment upon any of the preceding heads. Let all these smaller points stand aside. Let them never come into sight. 'If thine heart is as my heart,' if thou lovest God and all mankind, I ask no more: 'give me thine hand.'"[14] Here is the "Catholic Spirit" of the Wesleys and the "Caution against Bigotry"; and both sermons need to be repreached in our generation, lest we be found guilty of "that miserable bigotry which makes many so unready to believe that there is any work of God but among themselves."[15] Wesley knew, of course, to distinguish between "he that is not against us is for us" (Luke 9:50) and "he that is not with me is against me" (Luke 11:23). "A catholic spirit is not speculative latitudinarianism, it is not indifference to all opinions; secondly, it is not any kind of practical latitudinarianism, it is not indifference as to public worship, or as to the outward manner of performing it; thirdly, it is not indifference to all congregations—another sort of latitudinarianism, no less absurd and unscriptural than the former."[16] Paul and Apollo had each, no doubt, very determined views of his own about evangelism and church organization in Corinth; they thought it best to work separately, planting and watering in turn (I Corinthians 3:6; 16:12), recognizing each other as "but ministers, by whom ye believed," and apparently not demanding supplementary ordinations to "regularize" their "exchange of pulpits." On the other hand, by "schisms" in I Corinthians 11, as Wesley observes in the *Notes*, "is not meant any separation from the church, but uncharitable divisions in it; . . . there was no separation of any one party from the rest, with regard to external communion. . . . Therefore, the indulging any temper contrary to this tender care of each other is the true scriptural schism. . . . Both heresy and schism, in the modern sense of the

14. *Works*, V.499.
15. *Works*, VIII.257.
16. Ibid., V.502.

words, are sins that the Scripture knows nothing of; but were invented merely to deprive mankind of the benefit of private judgment, and liberty of conscience."[17]

Catholic love is a catholic spirit;[18] catholic Christianity, according to Acts 2:42, "consisted in these four particulars: hearing the word; having all things common; receiving the Lord's Supper; prayer."

> Ye different sects, who all declare,
> Lo, here is Christ, and Christ is there,
> Your stronger proofs divinely give,
> And show me where the Christians live![19]

This test reveals the great divide between the true and the false Church, Israel after the spirit and after the flesh (Romans 2:28–9, Galatians 4:29); it is the measure of the genuine apostolic succession and the judgment upon every mere "form of godliness" (II Timothy 3:5):

> The Church—alas! where is she to be found?
> Not in the mean, however dignified,
> Who would her creeds repeat, her laws deride,
> Her Prayers expunge, her Articles disown,
> And thrust the Filial Godhead from His throne.[20]

"Ye shall not cry much: Church, Church, Church!—ye shall prove that ye are the Church" (Luther).[21] Wesley is in good company. Apostles and Reformers are on his side, and he has no reason to fear the label "sectarian" or "schismatic" any more than they. He calmly takes up "that other objection, that we divide the Church. Remember, the Church is the faithful people, or true believers. Now, how do we divide these? 'Why, by our societies.'

17. Wesley, *Notes on the New Testament* (I Corinthians 11:18).
18. *Works*, V.503
19. The full text of the hymn is in Wesley's (1780) *Hymn Book*, Nos. 16–17: "Primitive Christianity."
20. An Epistle to the Reverend Mr. John Wesley, *Poetical Works of John and Charles Wesley*, VI.55.
21. Luther, *Works (Weimar Edition)*, XXX.2.231, 16ff. Cf. Charles Wesley on Jeremiah 7:4 ("the temple of the Lord, the temple of the Lord, the temple of the Lord") in *Poetical Works*, X.16.

Very good. Now the case is plain. 'We divided them,' you say, 'by uniting them together.' Truly a very uncommon way of dividing?"[22] The last judgment will not fall along denominational lines, and the only question for Wesley is the final one: "I care not who is head of the Church, provided *you* be a *Christian!*"[23]

This was written by John to his nephew Samuel after his "perversion to Popery." It could be shown even in the Wesleys' relationship to Roman Catholics[24]—to the persons, of course, not the system—that the Methodists intended to be "the friends of all, the enemies of none." "Is there any other society in Great Britain or Ireland that is so remote from bigotry? So truly of a catholic spirit? So ready to admit all serious persons without distinction? Where, then, is there such another society in Europe? In the habitable world? I know none. Let any man show it me that can. Till then let no one talk of the bigotry of the Methodists."[25]

The proof is in the program for common action that must follow from such premises. A vast field opens before us here: cooperation of scholars who find, as did Wesley and Bengel before them, that their unity grows in the measure in which tradition and prejudice are cast aside and the sheep learn to heed the voice of the good shepherd; cooperation of evangelists who go out together, as in the British commando Campaigns, and in similar ventures everywhere; cooperation of missionaries who discover for us the ABC of the Christian faith and compel the "old" Churches to sit at the feet of the "young." But greater still than common action is common suffering, through which, as Niemöller used to say, "we are beaten together," and in which, across all divisions and against all conventions, it suddenly is possible to ask with Wesley: "Is thy heart herein as my heart? If it be, give me thine hand." And in that moment, all our preliminary questions and disputes have lost their relevance.

22. *Works*, VIII.35, also p. 321.
23. *Letters*, VIII.47.
24. See *Letters*, III.7ff., "To a Roman Catholic"; *Works*, XI.194f., from "A Word to a Protestant."
25. *Works*, XIII.233. Cf. Charles Wesley's *Journal* of 8th September 1748: "In Kinsdale I am of every religion. The Presbyterians say I am a Presbyterian; the church-goers, that I am a Minister of theirs; and the Catholics are sure I am a good Catholic in my heart."

Where there is real urgency, true union will not wait; but without reformation there can be no reunion. All Saints' Day, November 1st, which John Wesley treasured so much, and which in its collect speaks of the "one communion and fellowship in the mystical body of Christ our Lord," is preceded in the calendar by Reformation Day, October 31st, the date of Luther's *Ninety-five Theses.* It cannot be otherwise. The end of the one Church must be reached by the same means of grace which, according to Luther and Wesley, are indispensable for the individual's salvation; and by the grace that operates these means, it will be reached.

First, prayer. "Again I say unto you, that if two of you shall agree on earth as touching any thing that they shall ask, it shall be done for them of my Father which is in heaven" (Matthew 18:19). South India has taught us that object lesson; there it has been demonstrated how unity came, not by ecclesiastical diplomacy and machination, but in answer to the prayers of the people who earnestly craved for it. As they were agreed in their desire, so they have become agreed in their worship—of which the new liturgy of the Church of South India gives impressive evidence. If we mean what we say in our petitions, we shall not be content to pray for one another, but go on to praying with one another and so discover our true common ground. The joint study of Methodists and Episcopalians, published in America in 1952, and setting forth, in factual synopsis, the rituals of the two Churches,[26] is therefore to be welcomed as a big step in the right direction.

It is surely more hopeful and challenging to be reminded of the same "Common Prayer," which in so large a measure is already accepted and used in our two communions side by side, than to engage in fruitless negotiations about the dry bones of our different episcopates. And in the joint study and devotional practice of our common heritage, we may well say, as did German Lutherans and Calvinists in the hour of their united witness at the Barmen Synod of 1934: "We leave to God what this may mean for the future relationship of the two denominations."

26. "A Study by the Protestant Episcopal Joint Commission on Approaches to Unity and The Methodist Commission on Church Union for presentation to the 1952 General Convention and the 1952 General Conference."

Second, the scriptures. We have already referred to the unifying effect of biblical research in our generation; nobody, reading a good commentary, would care to ask to which denomination the author might belong. It is the Word, in the great "ecumenical" seventeenth chapter of St. John, through which alone Christ's prayer for His church will be fulfilled; for by the Word the disciplines are distinguished from the word (verses 8, 14), by the Word they are preserved (11, 15) and sanctified (17,19), by the Word they bring the world to believe (20ff.), and by the Word they are made perfect in one (23). There is one body and one spirit, one hope of our calling, one Lord, one faith, one baptism, one God and Father of all (Ephesians 4:4–6); but there are "differences of administrations" and "diversities of operations" (I Corinthians 12:5–6) under the same Lord. Not one Bishop; nor even one Hymn Book. Sometimes the ecumenical discussion seems in danger of reversing the New Testament order of priority, forcing into one what the Spirit has left free, and scattering what He has gathered.

Third, the sacraments. They have their place, as we have seen, among the means of Wesley's evangelism; they are equally vital as means of true catholicity. We acknowledge one Baptism for the remission of sins; why not, in our different administrations, one communion as converting ordinance, instituted by our dying Lord, that we may be one in Him? If the cry over "the tragedy and scandal of our divisions" is serious, can it be coupled with the imposition of purely parochial conditions by the one side upon the other? If intercommunion is possible in colleges, hospitals, military services, wartime emergencies, and prison camps (e.g., Niemöller in Dachau, 1945), can any human authority prevent it under "normal" conditions? If we profess to believe in the real presence of our Lord in the blessed Sacrament, have we any time or right to inquire into the pedigree of the celebrant? If the comfortable words mean what they say, who can dare to keep himself or others away from His Table?

"Irregular" is the bogy that is raised against us here. "I am sure it was the will of God, but you must promise that it will never happen again" was, so we are told, the reaction of a high dignitary of the Episcopal Church to the news of an open intercommunion. The Conference of 1775 foresaw "that if His Grace

80

does not condescend to grant this request, Mssers Wesley will be obliged to take an irregular (not unevangelical) step and to ordain . . . ";[27] and Charles Wesley gave his own interpretation to the word in commenting upon Eldad and Medad who "went not out into the tabernacle, and prophesied in the camp" (Numbers 11:26ff.):

> Eldad, they said, and Medad there
> Irregularly bold,
> By Moses uncommission'd date
> A separate meeting hold!
> And still whom none, but Heaven, will own,
> Men whom the world decry,
> Men authorized by God alone
> Presume to prophesy![28]

To wait for an official permit before we break the bread together is to wait indefinitely; to wait until we are visibly one is the same error and sin as to wait till we are worthy. It is to waste the means of grace, to grieve the Holy Spirit, and to distrust the promise of Christ. "Irregularly bold" is the only attitude to take for those who are in earnest about reunion.

There is a further, specifically Methodist, way of "crossing the borders" which divide the Church; it is the itinerancy of the ministers. After all that may be said against it, and I have said it plainly in the previous chapter, there is still a case for the defense. Extend the circuit system beyond the boundaries of one country, let the mobility of the preachers be on a global scale, and you have a new practical aspect of catholic Christianity. When you are transferred, for instance, as I was, from one circuit of the universal Church (the German Lutheran) to another (the British Methodist) with no more ceremony to mark the occasion than is known at any "ordinary" change of states inside the British Connections (no reordination, no supplementary commission, and not even a local induction), then you learn to appreciate Wesley's catholic view of the Ministry, and the New Testament meaning of "recognition"—which is not the secular

27. *Journal,* VIII.333.
28. *Poetical Works,* IX.70.

admission or concession made by one side to the other, but the mutual "knowing" of ourselves as brothers in the family and through the likeness of Jesus Christ, our Lord.

Last, but not least, Charles Wesley's human again. Nowhere else in Christendom can they sing, as the Methodist people can (or could!), about the nature and the glory of the one, holy, catholic and apostolic Church. Here is the impulse to reunion in the bidding of God Himself:

> Let us join—'tis God commands—
> Let us join our hearts and hands;
> Help to gain our calling's hope,
> Build we each the other up. . . . [29]

Here is the criterion of our coming together in the hearing of the Word:

> Touched by the loadstone of Thy love,
> Let all our hearts agree,
> And ever toward each other move,
> And ever move toward Thee.[30]

Here is the true church, purified by fire, marked by the cross, set apart from the world, in phrases that might well have been coined in twentieth-century Europe:

> All are not lost or wandered back;
> All have not left Thy Church and Thee;
> there are who suffer for Thy sake,
> Enjoy Thy glorious infamy,
> Esteem the scandal of the cross,
> And only seek divine applause.[31]

But as real as that great divide is the family bond between those militant here on earth and those triumphant in heaven:

> One family we dwell in Him,
> though now divided by the stream,

29. *M.H.B.*, No. 713.
30. Ibid., No. 721.
31. Ibid., No. 737.

The narrow stream of death:
One army of the living God,
To His command we bow;
Part of His host have crossed the flood,
And part are crossing now.[32]

And here is the vision of the final consummation:

Love, like death, hath all destroyed,
Rendered all distinctions void;
Names, and sects, and parties fall:
Thou, O Christ, art all in all.[33]

What would any future Church union be in which, as is only too likely, these hymns might no longer be sung? What would it profit us to gain yet bigger numbers by another merger with the right or the left, if we lost the soul of Methodism? "God did raise up the Methodist people," a friend once wrote to me, "to proclaim, to all who would hear, the message which you have found in the Wesley hymns. As a Church, all too truly in recent years, we have been missing our providential way. Yet if we fail, there is no other Church in this land (nor, I think, overseas) which has the burden of this word laid upon it. I am keen on reunion, but not by absorption into theological illiteracy or evangelical forgetfulness. I want to see a reunion in which all of us bring together, and share with one another, our treasures. And, under God, we have our treasures to bring." Catholic Christianity, according to the Wesleys, is not a diluted Gospel, a getting-together of the Churches on the basis of the lowest common denominator; it is, on the contrary, an approach to reunion in which the Methodist identity is preserved. We have no reason to hide, and every reason to publish, in the several senses of that word, our hymns (in Wesley's edition!), our forms of service, devotional and practical, and, above all, our doctrinal standards, the *Notes* and the *Sermons*, so that we may know and make known the things for which we stand.

The Methodist identity preserved—can this be briefly defined? The answer seems to me to lie each time in the doctrine

32. *M.H.B.*, No. 824.
33. Ibid., No. 720.

of the Holy Spirit. Scriptural Christianity, for Wesley, is the fullness of Christ made manifest in the Holy Spirit, who dwells in the heart of the believer and in the body of the Church; the lesson which preceded the first of these lectures was taken from Romans 10, for it was St. Paul who taught the Wesleys the Scripture Way of Salvation. Practical Christianity is the doing of the Word, written by the Spirit upon the fleshy tables of the heart, and embodied in the life of the new covenant; the lesson at that lecture was from the conclusion of the Sermon on the Mount, representing the synoptic part of the New Testament. Missionary Christianity is the "distribution of the merits of Christ," by the ordinary and extraordinary means of evangelism, aiming at the "perfect man of God," who is the product of the Word, and whose entire holiness is the work of the sanctifying Spirit; here the lesson was from the *Acts of the Apostles* (Chapter 2) which we found illustrated in Wesley's *Journal*. Catholic Christianity is the catholic Spirit in action, the Spirit as the author and bond of unity, freeing us from the law and guiding us into all truth; the lesson at this last lecture came from John 17 in completion of the scriptural witness.

Another possible summary could be found in the seven letters of Revelation 2–3, many details of which are "annotated" by the message of the Wesleys in the way suggested by our earlier brief analysis of Romans. Each of these letters ends with the words: "He that hath an ear, let him hear what the Spirit saith unto the churches." That is exactly what John and Charles Wesley would say to us today. And if we have ears to hear, we shall respond in the prayer that many Methodists use in Britain and that may also serve here as a concluding reminder (1, 2, 3, 4) of this course:

> Almighty God, (1) who didst raise up Thy servants John and Charles Wesley to proclaim anew the gift of redemption and the life of holiness, (2) be with us, their children, and revive Thy work among us, that (3) inspired by the same faith and upheld by the same grace in word and sacrament, (4) we and all Thy people may be made one in the unity of Thy Church on earth, even as in heaven we are made one in Thee; through Jesus Christ our Lord. Amen.

Subject Index

Methodist: A Survey of the Christian Way (Carter) 33
Methodist Church 32
  activism of 37
  history of 34
  in America 13, 73, 74
  practices of 35
  principles of 34, 35
Methodist Hymn-Book (Charles Wesley)
  No. 3130
  No. 8921
  No. 9021
  No. 9756
  No. 23257
  No. 24356
  No. 24823
  No. 26348, 61
  No. 27050, 56
  No. 28432
  No. 31022
  No. 34439
  No. 34723
  No. 36161
  No. 38341
  No. 38465
  No. 38663
  No. 39941
  No. 41156
  No. 41256
  No. 43167
  No. 48156
  No. 53020
  No. 56157
  No. 57238, 46
  No. 57832
  No. 59432
  No. 59832
  No. 60542
  No. 66156
  No. 71382
  No. 72083
  No. 72182
  No. 73782
  No. 76157
  No. 76558
  No. 76758
  No. 78358
  No. 82483
  No. 87438
  No. 88122
Methodist Society 24, 43
Methodist Synod 73, 74
Methodists 13–15, 20, 24, 25, 27, 33–38, 40, 48, 55, 58, 69–72, 78, 79, 82–84
  in America 32, 36, 72, 74
  in Britain 36, 81
  in Germany 36
  preaching to the Irish, in 1753 48
  preservation of their identity 83
Missionary Christianity 47, 84
Moore 17
Moravian Diaries 18
Moravian Quietism 37
Moravians 15
Moses 45, 72, 81
Mystic Purgatory 63, 65
Mystical experience 27

Nantwich 48
Nationalism 33
Nazareth 29
New Testament 15, 18, 22, 24–26, 28, 30, 43, 44, 51, 56, 62, 64, 66, 80, 81, 84
Nicolson, Roy S. 64
Nicolson Square Church, Edinburgh 16
Niemöller 78, 80
Ninety-Five Theses (Luther) 79
Nomism 45
Notes on the New Testament (John Wesley) 20, 21, 26, 27, 34, 44, 54, 76, 77, 83

Old Religion 16
Old Testament 22, 24, 26, 44, 51, 64
Oratio-meditatio-tentatio 26
Our Threatened Values (Gollancz) 33
Oxford 27, 53

Paraclete 29, 30
Pastoral Epistles 15
Paul, St. 25, 29, 34, 44, 45, 59, 60, 72, 74, 76, 84
Pauline Theology 56, 58, 60
Pauline Vocabulary 14

Scripture Index

Franz Hildebrandt studied at Tübingen and Berlin and served as the vicar of Martin Niemoller during the early struggle of the Confessing Church against Hitler. A refugee from the Third Reich, he completed his Ph.D. at Cambridge University, later serving as a pastor in Cambridge and Edinburgh and as professor of Christian theology at Drew University. He wrote *Melanchthon: Alien or Ally, From Luther to Wesley,* and *I Offered Christ.* He also served as co-editor of the critical edition of the hymns of John and Charles Wesley.